Plate 1 Pitt, father and son in early life

The Journey from
Blandford to Hayes

ANNE MANNING

The lives and times of two Prime Ministers,
William Pitt (Earl of Chatham) and William Pitt the Younger

GW00602744

THE LONDON BOROUGH

BROMLEY LIBRARIES 2009

FIRST PUBLISHED IN 2009

by
Bromley Libraries
Central Library
High Street
Bromley BR1 1EX
020 8461 7170

ISBN 978 0 901002 20 4

Printed by CPI Antony Rowe

CONTENTS

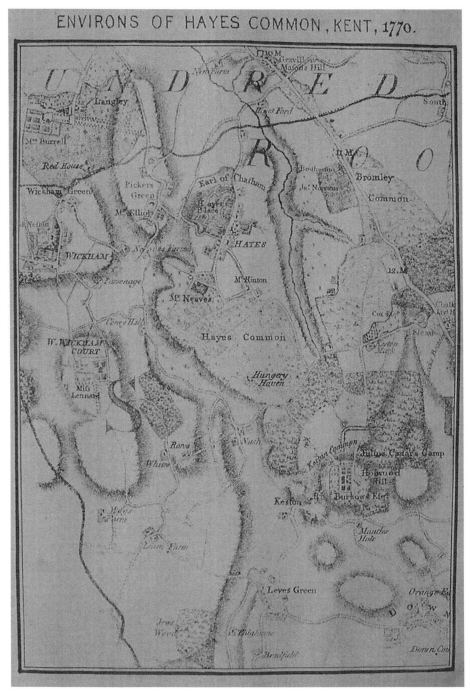

Plate 2 Map of Hayes area, c1770

INTRODUCTION

The villages of Hayes, Keston and West Wickham, now part of the London Borough of Bromley, have been home over the centuries to many influential people from the worlds of finance, business, industry and politics. Their close proximity to London but quiet rural nature made them ideal places for country retreats, for those who could afford such luxuries, from the time that London became established as the nation's capital. After the electrification of the railways their role changed, becoming comfortable suburbs within easy reach of city offices and workplaces.

A surprising number of former Prime Ministers have had connections with areas now in Bromley Borough. Harold Macmillan, (Prime Minister from 1957 to 1963) was MP for Bromley from 1945 to 1964 and Andrew Bonar Law, (Prime Minister from 1922 to 1923) was MP for Dulwich from 1906 to 1910 which at the time included Penge. Margaret Thatcher, (Prime Minister from 1979 to 1990), lived at Farnborough Park at the start of her political career, while her successor as PM, John Major (1990 to 1997), was active in Beckenham politics in his early career. The two most closely associated with the local area though were the two Pitts, William Pitt the elder, Earl of Chatham, Prime Minister from 1757 to 1761 and again from 1766-1768 whose love of Hayes, once established, never diminished and his son, Pitt the younger, PM from 1783 to 1801 and 1804 to 1806, the only Prime Minister to be born here.

It is not entirely clear when, why and how the Pitt family became linked to Hayes. William Pitt the Elder, Earl of Chatham, was friends with Revd Gilbert West, a poet, who lived at The Grove[1] in West Wickham, and with Mrs Elizabeth Montague, a leading member of the Blue Stockings[2], who leased Hayes Place. Pitt visited them both and, on seeing Hayes Place, fell in love with it, so much so that he managed to buy the house in 1756. With the exception of a short break in the 1760s, Pitts lived either at Hayes Place or at Holwood in nearby Keston, for close on 50 years.

Many books have been written about this father and son, primarily from the viewpoint of their influential contributions to the political life of this country. The close proximity of the tercentenary of the birth of Pitt the

1 Later Ravenswood
2 See picture caption on page 34

Elder on 15th November 1708 and the 250th anniversary of the birth of Pitt the Younger on 28th May 1759, however, has provided an opportunity to mark their lives in Hayes and Keston, yet still within the political and historical context of the time.

Some understanding of politics in the 18th century will help to make sense of this journey.

- This was a period when the monarch still had major influence in the running of the country, the ruling administration being known as the King's Party. This was a time when Kings of England did not always get on with their heirs and consequently the Princes of Wales would often take charge of the Opposition.

- The monarch was able to dictate who should be part of his government. Pitt the Elder did not enjoy the support of the King in the early part of his career and, thus, was in his late forties before he obtained a senior position.

- There were two parties, the Whigs and the Tories, but they were not political parties as we know today. There was little difference between the aims of the parties. Much depended on whether or not you supported the King and/or individuals within the Administration. Members of either party could be in the administration, even in the Cabinet. Pitt the Elder was a Whig, while Pitt the Younger was usually considered to be a Tory, but claimed to be an Independent Whig.

- While the Parliamentary system of government of the time was a fair one, the methods of becoming an elected representative (a Member of Parliament) left much to be desired. Pocket (or Close) and Rotten Boroughs ruled the day across much of the country. Such Boroughs were often owned or controlled by individuals – landowners and those with much influence – and the number under their control wasn't restricted. Many of these seats had few electors, and the seats and the electors could be bought. There was little campaigning outside some of the big counties, such as Yorkshire, London and Middlesex. Seats such as Old Sarum, owned and represented by the Pitt family, had around only a handful of electors yet returned two MPs, while Manchester – a burgeoning town –

had none, represented simply as part of Lancashire. This situation had not been planned but had come about through a state of inertia.

- Significant changes were not introduced until the Reform Act 1832, despite the attempts made by Pitt the Younger in the 1780s.

- Prime Ministers, as we know them today, were not truly official appointments until the time of Lord Salisbury (Prime Minister 1885-86 and 1894-1902). First or Chief Minister was the more common title at the time. Robert Walpole (PM 1721-42), however, was described as Prime Minister at the time. [Pitt the Elder, although acknowledged by many, including the author of this book, as Prime Minister between 1757 and 1761, officially shared control of the government with the Duke of Newcastle, with the latter taking the formal title of PM.]

- Prime Ministers were almost always the First Lord of the Treasury. Pitt the Elder, was an exception.

- *Hansard* is the 'in-house' record of Parliamentary proceedings and it was first produced in 1803. For some time prior to that year, there were other versions of the proceedings. However, it was an infringement of Parliamentary privilege for anyone to publish any record of the proceedings. A change in the privileges came about in 1771 as a result of the role played by a Bromley resident – Brass Crosby – who lived at Chelsfield. Crosby was a Magistrate, MP for Honiton from 1768 and had been Lord Mayor of London in 1770. Crosby was ordered to come before the House of Commons, following his release of a printer who had come before him in court and who had dared to publish reports of Parliamentary proceedings. The House committed Crosby to the Tower of London. But, when Crosby was brought to trial, several judges refused to hear the case and, after protests, he was released. No further attempts were made to prevent publication.

CHAPTER 1

The Pitts and their immediate origins

The journey begins at Blandford St. Mary, Dorset the birthplace of Thomas Pitt, the grandfather of William Pitt the Elder, as it was he who probably had the greatest influence on the future development of the two Pitts, both of whom became Prime Minister. Various traits of his appeared in future generations and he was the first of this branch of the Pitt family to enter Parliament.

The Pitts, at this stage, were considered to be little more than lesser English gentry, Lord Rosebery telling us that the Pitt family was gentle and honourable, taking two centuries to grow into wealth, without producing anything illustrious. However, everything changed in the 18th century, when the family took off, blossoming into four peerages – Londonderry, Rivers, Camelford and Chatham – none of which survive today.

It was through grandfather Thomas that the name of Pitt first came into prominence. He was born on 5th July 1653, the son of Robert Pitt, Vicar of Blandford, and grandson of Thomas Pitt, a physician.

Thomas was thought to have started his working life as a sailor, before becoming an illicit merchant or an interloper, carrying on trade in violation of the East India Company's monopoly. It was in this trade that Thomas made his first fortune. In fact, Thomas drove that company to despair. In order to keep him on a tight rein he was given the position of Governor of Fort St George, in Madras, which he governed with a strong hand from 1698. However, by 1709 the Company decided it had had enough of Thomas Pitt and dismissed him.

Thomas returned to England but was soon back in India, where he purchased a large diamond, later known as the Pitt Diamond, which helped to put the family on a good financial footing.

Long before these events around 1680, Thomas had married Jane, daughter of James Innes of Reid Hall, Moray. They had six children, one of whom, named William, died in infancy. The surviving children were Robert (father of Pitt the Elder), Thomas, John, and two daughters, Essex and Lucy. Thomas was to become the 1st Lord Londonderry; John became a soldier of distinction and was ADC (Aide-De-Camp) to the King – probably George II; Essex married Charles Cholmondley, while Lucy made a great match, marrying James

Stanhope, who became an important general and the 1st Earl of Stanhope. The Stanhopes feature at many points in the lives of the two Williams.

Thomas was a lively person, described variously as intrepid and formidable, a difficult servant, energetic, self-reliant, and haughty, with a temper. It is also said that he displayed irrational feelings towards, not only his children, but also towards his wife, pouring on them his scorn and invective – going so far as advising his children to have nothing to do with their mother. There seems to have been an element of madness in his character and, over the years, many have inferred that grandson William, and other descendants of Thomas, had similar traits. However, he had a fondness for his grandson William, taking him to and from college at Eton. In fact, he described William as a "hopeful lad, and doubt not but he will deliver yours and all his friends' expectations".

Returning to England permanently in 1710, two years after William's birth, Thomas sold the diamond to the French monarchy. It was with the money gained from the sale of this stone that he was able to buy Boconnoc in Cornwall in 1717. He also purchased a large number of other properties, many

1 Boconnoc House, Lostwithiel, Cornwall, bought by Thomas Pitt in 1717

of which feature in William the Elder's life, including;- The Down House at Blandford St. Mary; Kynaston and Woodyates in Dorset; Bradock, Treskilliard and Brannell, all in Cornwall; Abbot's Ann (Hampshire); Swallowfield Park (Berkshire), his favourite; and Mawarden Court at Stratford–sub–Castle in Wiltshire.

2 The Down House, Blandford St Mary. Home of Thomas Pitt

From this period onwards, Thomas was known as Diamond Pitt or Governor Pitt. The diamond, later known as the Regent Diamond, having been sold to the French Prince Regent, was said to have been set in Napoleon's sword[1].

Despite these various activities abroad, Thomas found time to pursue other lines of occupation and entered Parliament in 1689 – the first in this line of the Pitts to enter Parliament - representing Old Sarum, a notorious Rotten Borough with only a handful of voters and was re-elected for the same seat the following year. To achieve this, he had bought the manors of both Stratford sub Castle and Old Sarum from Lord Salisbury. Further re-elections followed in 1714 and 1715 along with his son Robert, Old Sarum having two seats. In 1717 Thomas was elected to serve Thirsk, having vacated his Old Sarum seat to take up the post of Governor of Jamaica, although in the end he wasn't appointed, returning to represent his original constituency in 1722.

Having a seat in the House of Commons, if for no other reason, required Thomas to have somewhere to live in London. Various references have been made to him being in Pall Mall and St James's Street, both within the Parish of St James's, Westminster.

---

1 However, David Nash Ford, on the Royal Berkshire History website, http://www.berkshirehistory. com/bios/tpitt.html, states that it was placed in the French crown. Today it is to be found in the Louvre.

Thomas did not restrict his purchasing interests to areas of grand houses. Much of Mayfair and Soho was still in the process of being developed and he acquired leasehold interests in Dean Street in Soho, known as the Pitt Estate, now the centre of the film industry, the freehold being owned by the Crown. The leasehold interests passed down through the family but were later assigned in 1765 to Sir Thomas Wilson of Wickham Court, near to Hayes.

Thomas Pitt died in 1726 at Swallowfield and was buried at Blandford St. Mary. His estate was the subject of litigation, an event not unusual in the history of the Pitt family.

Thomas' son Robert seems to have been of a totally different character to his father. He was well educated, as were all his siblings, Governor Pitt

3 Robert Pitt, father of William Pitt, Earl of Chatham

considering education to be of great importance, even for girls. He like his father, became a Member of Parliament, representing Old Sarum and Thirsk at various times. No doubt due to his father's treatment of the family, and perhaps the attention showered on young William, Robert comes across as being of a rather weak character. His only achievement of any note appears to have been his appointment as the Clerk of the Board of Green Cloth, an appointment involving the organisation of visits and helping to run the household of the Prince of Wales. In addition, he helped the Prince of Wales, in his role as the Duke of Cornwall, with estate and political matters in the west country.

Robert is often referred to in books as being 'of Boconnoc'. This certainly was true at the time of his death; however, the property would only have come into his hands at the time of his father's death the year before. Boconnoc, near Lostwithiel, is one of the great houses of Cornwall and it played an earlier role in the history of England, having been King Charles I's headquarters in the Civil War[1].

Robert, with his marriage to Harriet Villiers in 1703, brought into the family many major connections, including the Grenvilles, the Temples of Stowe

4 Harriet Pitt, nee Villiers, wife of Robert

and the Grandisons, many of whom played leading roles in Parliament, government and society generally. Various members of these families were to be closely involved in the lives and careers of both William Pitts, not always to their advantage.

Robert's life was a short one, dying only a year after his father, in 1727. Like his father, his estate was subject to many family squabbles and court litigation. He and Harriet produced seven children. Five were girls – Harriot, Mary, Ann, Catherine and Elizabeth – with Ann playing an important role in the life of brother William. Thomas his elder son made an important marriage, his wife, Christian, being the daughter of Sir Thomas Lyttleton. Their eldest child became the first Lord Camelford.

---

1 The house stands in lovely grounds, which are occasionally open to the public. Boconnoc was sold around 1820 to the Fortescue family, who still own it today.

5 The probable site of Pitt the Elder's birth, 28 Golden Square in 2008, now Sony Pictures Europe

6 A typical 18th century house in Golden Square. No. 28 probably originally looked similar

CHAPTER 2

William Pitt the Elder, Earl of Chatham

His Early Life

HOUSE OF EARL CHATHAM (EXTERIOR).

William was born on 15th November 1708 in Westminster, almost certainly at No. 28 Golden Square[1] the home of his father[2]. Within a month, on 13th December, he was baptised at St James's, Piccadilly. His godparents are said to have been Cousin Pitt – probably George Pitt of Strathfieldsaye[3] – and General William Stewart, after whom he was named. The General was the second husband of William's maternal grandmother, Lady Grandison.

7 Cutting from the Kadwell Portfolio in Bromley Archives, giving an alternative location for Pitt's birth, 44-45 Orchard Street

1 The survey of London Vol. XXXI, Part II, p.161; states that Robert Pitt occupied No. 28 Golden Square in 1708.
2 However the Kadwell Portfolio in Bromley Archives (Ref P/180/28/13) contains an uncredited cutting stating that he was born in Orchard Street, Westminster, later Nos. 44/45, now Abbey Orchard Street in a house demolished in the 1840s to make way for the building of Victoria Street. No other reference to this address has been traced,
3 Later Stratfield Saye, home of the Dukes of Wellington.

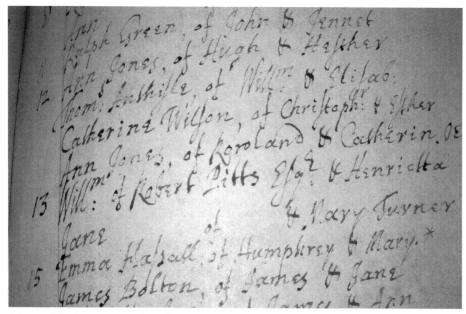

8 Copy of the baptism entry for William Pitt the Elder from the registers of St. James's Church, Piccadilly

9 Mawarden Court, Stratford sub Castle, Wiltshire; main childhood home of Pitt the Elder

The family owned a number of properties, which passed to William's father on his grandfather's death. William would have spent time in most of them. Mawarden Court, at Stratford-sub-Castle in Wiltshire, features more than most and was described as 'home'. It seems that William was at Mawarden during the 1715 Jacobite rebellion, when an uprising was expected in the West Country which must have been very exciting for the young child. William's parents were taking no chances with the safety of their children however and, while Robert went to organise the militia in nearby Blandford, all were despatched to the care of their grandmother, Lady Grandison, in St James's, London. Grandfather Thomas was also at St James's at the time – he had a home in Pall Mall - providing him with a good opportunity to get to know his grandchildren.

As has been mentioned earlier, Governor Pitt viewed William with some favour, realising that he had potential but grandfather's favours did not extend to money and, after his death, he provided William with an annuity of only £100 a year (£150,000 in today's money), a fortune for most people but disappointing for William considering his grandfather's vast wealth. This was all that came to William as his father, apparently, left him nothing other than the income from a few rents.

William's time at Eton College was not a happy one. Although he came from a wealthy family, he was placed on the foundation as a King's Scholar and not allowed to enjoy an easy life. He was flogged for being out of bounds, and severely so, and he was to suffer the hardships of the Long Chamber, a large dormitory with, it seems, awful traditions. According to Lord Shelburne William is said later to have claimed that he had hardly come across a boy who was not cowed for life at Eton.

These feelings may well have been shared by fellow pupils but William was an academic success, so much so that his tutor, William Burchett, wrote to his father in 1722, noting the progress he was making and acknowledging that he never had any concerns with this pupil who had good abilities and was of a good disposition. In fact, Mr Burchett closes by saying "there is no question to be made but he will answer all y'r hopes".

William made some good friends while at Eton, one of whom, George Lyttleton, was to remark during their school days of William's good humour and genius, a rare comment for one pupil to make of another. Another contemporary was Henry Fox. William is said to have been a bit of a recluse but his time at Eton, which came to an end in 1726, although unhappy, no doubt helped to form the man who was to become Prime Minister.

There was talk within the wider family, while still at Eton, that William was being lined up for the church. It seems that the parish of Abbot's Ann, Hampshire; one of Governor Pitt's purchases, was likely to become vacant. Until William was old enough, it could be 'cared for' by Christopher, the son of his father's cousin, Elizabeth, and incumbent at Pimperne, near Blandford as well as Chaplain to the 1st Earl of Stanhope. But no more seems to have been said about this possibility.

In 1726, at 18 years of age, William moved on to Trinity College, Oxford as a Gentleman Commoner. George Lyttleton also went to Oxford, where their friendship developed further. Among the acquaintances they made was Francis Ayscough, whose name will also occur again. William's time at Oxford is said by some to have been cut short due to ill health. It is more likely that the death of his father, Robert, in 1727 and the potential dependency on brother Thomas was the cause, the cost of being an undergraduate being high. William left the university within a year without a degree.

On leaving Oxford, William went to Utrecht in 1728 to complete his education, a not unusual step for young men at the time. Also there was his cousin Lord Villiers. While in Utrecht, William received a letter from George Lyttleton, his friend from Eton, telling William he had fallen in love with both Harriot and Ann Pitt, William's sisters; but nothing came of this as the Pitts, other than brother Thomas, had no money.

William's time in Utrecht appears to have been short-lived and in January 1730 he was in Boconnoc, now in the ownership of brother Thomas. Other times during this inactive period were, no doubt, split between other houses belonging to the family, such as the London town house in Pall Mall, and the other country residences at Swallowfield and Blandford, all purchased by Governor Pitt, with an occasional visit to Bath, where his mother frequently retired for the waters. A young man of limited means, he would need to lay his head somewhere!

Not being one to be idle, William began to gravitate towards the army, receiving a commission as a cornet[1] in February 1731 in the King's Own Regiment of Horse. No doubt William was encouraged during his childhood by his military uncle, the 1st Earl of Stanhope, to take this step but, more significantly, was influenced by Lyttleton's mother, sister to Lord Cobham, Colonel of the Regiment and distinguished veteran of the of the wars of the Duke of Marlborough. The Commission came at a cost of £1,000 – an enormous sum of money at that time, paid for by the Walpole administration and possibly by William's brother, Thomas. The Walpole link would have been a mark of favouritism, Thomas bringing the four seats he owned into the Parliament of 1727. The commission was confirmed in the March, by the kissing of hands with King George II, the monarch who later came to dislike Pitt.

---

1 The modern equivalent would be a second lieutenant, the lowest rank of commissioned officer in the army.

After "a long confinement in Quarters", William was back in Boconnoc by October 1731 bewailing the awful weather[1].

In 1733, although still in the army, William set out on his second foreign tour. Places he visited included Paris, Besançon, Marseilles, Montpelier, Lyon, Geneva, Strasbourg and Luneville. While in Besancon, William first lost his heart, introduced to the "finest woman here" who he had "the honour to dine with at her campagne,"[2] however it lead to nothing. As usual, he was in correspondence with his mother, who was living at the time in Bateman Street, Piccadilly. The letters, even though written some 6 years after his father's death, indicate that litigation over the latter's estate was not yet over. By 1734, William was back in England and returned to duty with his regiment in Newbury.

During this period, sister Ann had become a Maid of Honour to Queen Caroline, the wife of George II. Ann also became a member of a very distinguished group of ladies, both clever and idiosyncratic, the Blue Stockings, later getting to know Elizabeth Montague, one time leaseholder of Hayes Place. William and Ann were very close, unusually so for a brother and sister. This friendship began in their childhood and lasted for some years. Letters were to pass between them frequently – William addressing her as 'Nanny' and 'Little Jug' – and the lack of a letter would distress William enormously. However, their relationship was not always rosy, both having similar temperaments. Even though only in his middle 20s, William had already begun to advise, even dictate to, Ann about how she should lead her life; an approach which was to lead to acrimonious feelings between them in later years.

His Early Political Life

Although still a cornet, another major change was about to occur in William's life. On 18th February 1735 he was elected to sit in the House of Commons as one of the two Members for Old Sarum, succeeding his brother Thomas. Brother in-law, Robert Nedham, husband of sister Catherine, took the second Old Sarum seat. Thus began William's political life, one that was to last for 42 years.

Some weeks later, in July, he visited Stowe, the home of Lord Cobham, on one occasion even playing cricket. His stay was to last until December. In fact, Stowe was to be Pitt's home for about 3 years and became his second home. It was at Stowe that William was 'tutored' by Cobham, as were a number of other young men with political ambitions. 'Cobham's Cubs' was one name given to the group, another being 'the Cousins' as many were indeed cousins.

---

1 Letter to his mother Harriot dated 17.10.1731 as quoted by Rosebery, p.43-44.
2 Letter dated 5.6.1733 to his sister (probably Ann) as quoted by Rosebery p.70.

10 Old Sarum , 2008. The ruins visible here were excavated in the early 20th Century. In Pitt's day Old Sarum was simply a grassy hill used for grazing sheep.

11 Remains of the memorial to the parliament tree at Old Sarum. Prior to 1832 elections took place by electors and candidates visiting an appointed site within the constituency. At Old Sarum this was a tree at the foot of the castle mound, close to the site of the medieval town.

12 Stowe House, main front, 2008. The home of Stowe School since 1923

Stowe was probably where William was first introduced to what became his great passion (other than politics), that of gardening, from landscape design to the more practical elements. This aspect of life was becoming an acknowledged art form and owners of the great houses, such as Cobham at Stowe, pursued it avidly. William was a willing and interested student. He practised his art at many big houses during the 1740s and early '50s, the owners, many of whom were friends and/or relations, seeking out his expertise. William Warburton, Bishop of Gloucester, is even recorded as claiming that Pitt was superior to 'Capability' Brown in his designs[1].

In politics, William was a Whig and immediately joined the Opposition, whose leader at the time was Frederick, Prince of Wales.

He took a back seat for just a few weeks, doing little more than casting his vote when required. In April 1735, William made his maiden speech. He was joined in the debate by friend, George Lyttleton, and the sons of the Earl of Marchmont. They were all reckoned to have made a promising debut on the Opposition benches.

In the next session of Parliament, in 1736, William not only came to the attention of his fellow MPs but was to suffer the vengeance of the King. This happened on 29th April 1736 following an address of congratulation to the King on the recent marriage of the Prince of Wales.

1 Symes p.126

13 Stowe House cricket pitch 2008. Pitt the Elder played cricket at Stowe in 1735

14 Stowe Gardens, an inspiration to Pitt's garden designs

There was a great deal of animosity between the Hanoverian Kings and their heirs and William earned the approbation of the King. His commission was removed, an act of the King that was seen to be vindictive and an affront to the army. William, already someone to be noticed, decided to respond. He took to his one-horse chaise and rode around the country, attracting the attention of a great number of people. This may have been the first sign of the Great Commoner, as Pitt was to become known.

To make up for the loss of the cornetcy, and the pay that went with it, the Prince of Wales made William Groom of the Bedchamber. As an adviser to the Prince, William was also given the opportunity to meet various important bodies, including leaders of the City of London – a link that became increasingly important over the years.

Matters discussed in the House of Commons during these early years, all of which gave William opportunity to express his views, included:-

- the size of Britain's standing army;
- the second of the Jacobite Rebellions (1745);
- the financial support of Hanoverian troops;
- the combined roles of the King as monarch of Britain while also the Elector of Hanover;
- war with Spain, declared in 1739;
- the 'War of Jenkin's Ear';
- War of The Austrian Succession 1740-48;
- war with France (begun in 1744);
- Seven Years' War 1754-61.

In fact, Britain was at war for much of the next 24 years.

These various problems made Walpole, as Prime Minister, very vulnerable, so much so that in 1742 he resigned. A period of flux followed, resulting in Henry Pelham, brother of the Duke of Newcastle, becoming First Minister. Despite understanding that the role of Secretary of State for War might come his way, William did not receive any position. It so happened that he was in Bath at the time, seeking respite from a number of ailments, said to include gout of the bowels, as well as possibly depression. It could be that his absence did him no favours, although, with the improvement in his financial situation as a result of his appointment to serve the Prince of Wales, William may have concluded that a position was not necessary.

By 1744, William '... upon account of his merit in the noble defence he has made for the support of the laws of England, and to prevent the ruin of his country'[1] had met with the approval of Sarah, Duchess of Marlborough (widow of the renowned general), so much so that she bequeathed him the sum of

---

1 Ayling.p.90 quoting Thackerary's History of William Pitt, 1827.

£10,000 in her will. This inheritance was of great importance to William as he would now be in a position of financial independence.

The following year, William resigned from his position as Groom of the Bedchamber to the Prince of Wales, and thus took another step on the route to full independence.

Following various proposals to bring William into the government, all of which failed due to the King's opposition, he was offered and accepted, in 1746, the post of Vice-Treasurer of Ireland, a position that brought an income of £3,000 a year. Now being a member of the government, albeit in a minor role, William began to vote with the government and, consequently, for the King. This did not go unnoticed.

Soon after this appointment, William was appointed as Paymaster General, his predecessor having just died. These two positions, which he occupied for eight years, were somewhat of a backwater. However, the Paymaster's role was a positive move as it brought him into the Privy Council and the company of the King although he refused to speak to him for four years!

The Paymaster General position brought William a further income of £4,000 a year, an official residence in Whitehall and other perquisites. Mutterings about his independence and impartiality came to the fore. However, there was little to substantiate such accusations, as William rejected everything

15 Paymaster General's house, from Horse Guards Parade, 2008. The house is set back in the centre of this view

except the income and official home. In fact William ensured that it was widely known that he did so, Pitt "already saw that his power lay with the people, and that it was based not merely on his genius and eloquence, but on the faith in his public spirit and scrupulous integrity"[1].

As was standard practice at the time, William, having become a minister, was forced to give up his Parliamentary seat of Old Sarum. He turned to the Duke of Newcastle for help, who offered him the seat of Seaford in Sussex, a community of 70-80 householders. He won the seat, but only after the Duke gave the voters a dinner. This 'was the nearest Pitt ever came to fighting an election campaign'[2].

William, now apparently settled with a town house and a new seat, bought the lease in 1747 of a rural retreat, South Lodge, as his first real home.

16 South Lodge, Enfield Chase, Pitt's home from 1747

South Lodge was some miles out of London at Enfield Chase. Within the year, he had rebuilt the house – a regular occurrence with other houses he bought over the years - and created a park and pleasure grounds out of the surrounding fields, all at great cost. The works he undertook included creating a wooded island and rustic bridge, thereby enhancing the two existing lakes,

1 Rosebery p.258
2 Ayling p.115

plus the addition of various ornamental features. His friend Gilbert West praised his work and Mrs Elizabeth Montague, another visitor, rhapsodised over all that William had done. Some friends stayed to enjoy the shooting of game but most came to savour the visual delights that had been created. An authority on garden design, George Mason, commended Pitt's ability 'of making the interior correspond with the exterior scenery'[1]. Despite all this activity at South Lodge, Pitt spent no more than a week there at a time and, by 1752, he had had enough of the house and sold it.

Frequent references are made, then and since, as to William's presence. Physically, "he was tall, elegant and upright in character; his voice was clear and musical; his gestures studied and graceful; his general appearance commanding."[2]

In 1751 the Prince of Wales died, his son, aged 12 becoming heir to the throne. To allow for the appointment of a Regent in the event of him succeeding, a regency bill was introduced to Parliament. This caused a great deal of controversy and much fierce debate between Pitt and Henry Fox, another orator of quality in the house.

It was during this period that William began to show a change in his approach to the issues under discussion at the time. He acknowledged and atoned for the brashness of his youth, on one occasion pointing out, when he changed his stance on a particular issue, that he "was then very young and sanguine...I am now ten years older, and have had time to consider things more coolly". He had sown his wild oats and henceforward was to be regarded as a "prudent and sagacious statesman."[3]

The period after the elections of 1747 saw brother Thomas's financial situation, begin to deteriorate. He faced ruin and fled abroad in 1755 to escape his creditors. William stepped in to take responsibility for the education of Thomas's son, another Thomas and the future Lord Camelford, who was at Cambridge. This, and other input from William, however, earned him no thanks from young Thomas. Brother Thomas was eventually able to return to England, but only after his son settled his remaining debts, dying in 1761.

The early 1750s saw William spending more time, at Bath due to his health. Gout kept him constantly disabled and, despite now having homes elsewhere, Bath became almost his permanent abode. In 1753 he bought two houses in The Circus, at Nos. 7 (as an office and at a cost of £1,200) and 8 (to be his home), both under construction, having just sold South Lodge. He took up residence in 1754. This base in Bath became very much a political centre and

1 Symes p.128
2 Ayling p.106
3 Rosebery p284-5

17 No. 8 The Circus, Bath, 2008. Pitt's home from 1754

his cousin Philip, 2nd Lord Stanhope bought the house next door. William retained the properties until 1763[1].

Also in 1753, William spent time at Tunbridge Wells, accompanied by Gilbert West, his wife and sister Molly. Together they stayed at Stone House; but, despite the local waters, William's health deteriorated. Lyttleton came down to see William and West hoped that he would be able add his concerns to his own and persuade William to return to town and see a London physician. But William refused to do so. West's concerns were such that he wrote to Mrs Montague, to say that the doctors paid a lot of attention to William's bowel problems, rather than to the state of his mind – perhaps a more pressing problem. It may be the contents of this letter were what lead to Mrs Montague joining the party in Tunbridge Wells later in the summer. In any event, it would seem that William's health showed a turn for the better as Mrs Montague talks of them 'wandering about like a company of gypsies, visiting all the fine parks and seats in the neighbourhood'. After a five-day ride into Sussex, William returned to Tunbridge Wells, still suffering from insomnia, but well enough to attend lectures with Mrs Montague.

By mid-September, William had left the Wells and began his wanderings once more, possibly calling on Mrs Montague at Hayes Place[2], with the intention of returning to London in November for the start of the next Parliamentary session.

1 For more information see 'Let's join the Circus' In The Times 29/4/2005.
2 Rosebery p.306.

18 Stone House Tunbridge Wells, now Mount Ephrahim 2008 The house was substantially altered in the 1840s but is believed to be substantially the same building as that stayed in by Pitt in 1753.

The House was to see William, but only briefly, as he was soon back in Bath, very incapacitated by a serious attack of the more common version of gout. He was often unable to even get out of his chair, his feet being in such a bad way. He could not have picked a worse time to be so afflicted, as matters were coming to a head in London.

The First Minister, Pelham, died in March 1754. There followed a hectic few weeks of meetings and discussions about who should take Pelham's place, with letters flying frantically between the patient in Bath and London. Three possible contenders were all ruled out, William probably on account of his health, his connections and the attitude of the King towards him. In the end, the Duke of Newcastle, in the Lords, became the First Lord of the Treasury, ie First or Prime Minister. Other positions were handed to William's cousins, but nothing came William's way (although he held on to his Paymaster's job).

William, still tucked away in Bath, was bitter. While to some he advised that he would continue with his plan 'not to quit employments', to others he was talking about, even seeking, retirement. But his real friends were not taken in by his plea to be allowed to take a back seat, even to disappear. They each recognised that, while money was not of importance to William, the ambition remained.

But, unbeknownst to everyone, including William, his life was to take a sudden and major change.

Recovering from this long period of gout, by late summer William was out and about once more, staying at Astrop Wells in Northamptonshire, with a view to moving on to friends and family. For some reason, on leaving Astrop in early September, he suddenly changed his plans and decided to stay with his cousin George Grenville at Wotton House, Buckinghamshire, the Grenville family home. Within almost a matter of days, he had spoken to Hester Grenville, George's sister, and she had agreed to become his wife.

19 Wotton House Bucks. It was here while walking by the lake, Pitt proposed to his future wife.

It is hard to believe that William had made this decision on the spur of the moment. To do so would have been totally out of character; but he and Hester had known each other for many years – since her childhood – and for years he had been aware of her many attributes. It may be he had a mid-life crisis while in Astrop. He must have appreciated that his health was not good, his future prospects looked bleak, and he could not settle in any house, not even South Lodge. None of this made him the most attractive of suitors. Neither of them was young, he was 46 and she was 33; in fact, both would have been thought as middle-aged for the times they lived in. He must have concluded that he needed a wife; the question was put and the desired answer given.

This sense of urgency continued, William saying that he wished their wedding to take place around 6th or 7th of November, a week before the start of the next Parliamentary session. Hester was having none of that, saying that that allowed insufficient time to make all the necessary arrangements. However, Hester was soon back in London, at her lodgings in Argyll Street and everything was arranged. There were to be no Banns and a Special Licence or allegation was obtained for the wedding to take place at Hester's London residence on Saturday 16th November 1754.

The marriage service was taken by Rev'd Dr Francis Ayscough, a friend of William's from their university days, brother-in-law of George Lyttleton and chaplain to the Prince of Wales. It was a low key event, as William wished, with no Pitts present, the few guests being limited to Grenville relations. The couple left to spend their honeymoon at 'The Grove', the home of Gilbert West in West Wickham. Although Mrs Montague was at home at the time, at Hayes Place, barely a mile away, there was no contact as she was "unwilling to disturb, or interrupt the free course of those pleasures which ... are most relished when private"[1].

20 The licence or allegation authorising William and Hester Pitt's marriage.

1 Ayling p.150-1

21 Ravenswood House, West Wickham. William and Hester spent their honeymoon here as guests of Gilbert West in 1754 when it was still called Grove House. The house was demolished in two stages in the early twentieth century.

Despite the apparent suddenness of this marriage, it was recognised by everyone, family and friends, as a good match. Hester was to prove a great support to William while he, in his turn, was to show his great love for her, his many letters to her, although very flowery by modern standards, proving this to be the case. "Perhaps the only two unqualified successes in Pitt's life – but they were both resounding – were to be his conduct of the Seven Years War and his marriage to Hester Grenville"[1].

The Lead up to Power

In the meantime, trouble was brewing across the Atlantic, between the British colonists and the French, the colonists having been left very much to their own devices. The problems were in two areas, in New France (Canada) and in French Louisiana. The French built various forts, including Fort Du Quesne in 1754, by the Allegheny River. It was attacked by Lt Col George Washington but in July, at Fort Necessity, he had to surrender. The Seven Years' War, which could be said to be the first world war, its theatres including America, Europe, India as well as Africa, had begun.

Newcastle, the Prime Minister, was in a dilemma. Just weeks before Pitt's wedding, Newcastle was seeking William's views. William, although trying

1 Ibid p.151

to suggest that he had no role to play in such matters, advised the sending of artillery to America, and to be decisive.

This was the scene that awaited William on his return from honeymoon; major problems with the French, particularly In America; a government, within the Cabinet, that contained none of the best qualified people and the sense that he should be leading the country. William was ready to pounce, invigorated perhaps by his new found happiness at home.

The Prime Minister did not know which way to turn, faced with the possibility of an alliance of Pitt and Fox, Fox with his supporters in the Commons and Pitt , with his powerful mastery as a debater and orator. However, relations between Pitt and Fox deteriorated, so much so that Newcastle was able to get Fox on side, to some extent, and 'peace' reigned in the Commons through the early months of 1755; but news of the worsening situation in America brought home to Newcastle that Pitt was necessary to his needs. Various endeavours to persuade Pitt to come on board and, most importantly, to persuade the King to accept Pitt came to nought.

The months passed. Pitt suffered some ill health, but not sufficient to make him incapacitated. In October 1755, Hester had presented him with a daughter in London, another Hester, much to William's pleasure.

In November, a furious and withering debate, lead by William, erupted during the address on the King's speech. This lead to his dismissal from the government, with the loss of his income and the Paymaster's house. Fortunately, Lord Temple offered William an income of £1,000, which he accepted.

For nine years William had held a government position, although still outside the Cabinet. Whether he would be cast out into the wilderness remained to be seen but he was determined to continue to 'add to England's strength', and scarcely a day went by without him on his feet in the Commons. His jibes often found their quarry but he also was subjected to those directed at him. But, regardless, William could not be ignored and he continued to be the scourge of the government to the end of the session.

Despite all that surrounded him in the political field, William found time to spend Christmas 1755 in Bath, on his own, supervising the final works to his house there, much to the concern of Hester. She was worried about the expense, particularly as they now needed a town house. They soon found one in Brook Street. Not content with two houses, by early 1756, he had his eye on Hayes Place – a house in the country yet within easy reach of London.

Hayes was a small village, lying just 13 miles from Westminster and about two miles from the small market town of Bromley. Hayes Place was the principal house in the area and was sited in the heart of the village, opposite the parish church of St Mary the Virgin. There were a number of other large houses in the district, the occupiers of some of which were known to Pitt; Mrs Elizabeth Montague held a lease of Hayes Place, while Gilbert West lived only a mile away in West Wickham.

The area as whole was a rural one, with a great deal of farmland, some of which Pitt bought at various times so as to enlarge his estate and create a more private setting for the house. Also close by were a number of commons – Hayes, Keston and West Wickham – which, together with the farmland, provided opportunities for riding and other rural pursuits, ideal when bringing up a family. Clearly this was a house to suit William and his family and he bought Hayes Place in 1756.

At the time of purchase, Hayes Place comprised an old house and little grounds. Within a short time of moving in, William set to with his grandiose plans to build a new house, which took some time to complete. Over the

22 Hayes Place, an 18th century print.

next few years, he acquired various parcels of land surrounding the small estate bringing the acreage up to 40. Once more, William was able to put his gardening expertise into practise. He spent a lot of time at this task, with the help of his gardener, T Dally, his zeal being so over-powering that some planting was undertaken by torchlight[1]. Again, the compliments

---

1 Symes p129

flowed, from Hester – of course, Mrs Beckford, wife of the Lord Mayor of London, and Mrs Montague. Apparently, she returned to her former home in 1771, declaring at the time that it was so 'altered and so astonishingly improved since I lived there that I could almost accuse Lord Chatham of necromancy; he is *gran mago* and has called forth all the rural beauties from a spot which was once very unpromising. I wish you could see how sweet a pastoral scene he has made around him.[1]'

In the meantime, further problems were arising on the continent; the French had their eye on Minorca, then owned by Britain, and even contemplated an invasion of Britain. At home, William was urging the government to enlarge the navy – a force which he recognised would be very important to Britain's developing world role – and to create a large, home-based militia to take on the role of home defence. The French then invaded Minorca, beginning a siege of Port Mahon (Mahon being the name of the heir to the Stanhope earldom). The British forces arrived too late and Minorca was signed away on 14th July. The loss itself may not have been of great importance but Britain, through Admiral Byng, had lost the opportunity to do damage to the French fleet.

MRS. MONTAGU
"QUEEN OF THE BLUES"

23 *Elizabeth Montague, (1720-1800) Tenant of Hayes Place and friend of Pitt the Elder. She was the leader of the 'Bluestockings' a group of like-minded women and men who met to discuss literature, art, fashion and issues of the day.*

The situation over the summer of 1756 did not get any better, but William did not allow political problems to distract him from matters on the 'home front'. He was able to spend time at his new home in Hayes. The age and appearance

1 Ibid

of Hayes Place at that time is not recorded. Although it must have been pleasing – or perhaps it was the setting that appealed to him – plans would be soon in place to improve it. In the meantime, he enjoyed thoroughly his time at Hayes, even writing to George Grenville, his brother-in-law, about the 'pure air' of their village.

As summer moved into autumn, William was again in Hayes in time for the birth on 10th October 1756 of his first son, John. The clamour for Pitt, with or without Fox, to take control came from every direction, including the City of London. William was approached by Lord Hardwicke, on behalf of Newcastle. Pitt stood his ground, declining to serve with Newcastle. He also demanded direct access to the King. John was baptised at St Mary's, Hayes on 7th November.

William began to use every tactic open to him, and made approaches to Lady Yarmouth, the King's mistress. She was not unsympathetic. With Newcastle out of the way, following his resignation, on 27th October the King asked Fox to form a ministry. Fox, in turn, asked Pitt to join him. Pitt refused. The name of William Cavendish, The 4th Duke of Devonshire came into the arena, as a potential head of the Treasury (it so happens that Pitt had already passed Devonshire's name for the Treasury to Lady Yarmouth) and, by mid-November, a Devonshire-Pitt ministry was all but settled, with Pitt as Secretary of State for the Southern Department.[1] The seals were presented on 4th December 1756, and thus began Pitt's first ministry.

1756 to 1757 – Pitt-Devonshire Ministry

As a new Minister, Pitt was obliged once again to be re-elected to Parliament. Relations having broken down with the Duke of Newcastle, William felt that he could not retain Aldborough in Yorkshire which he had held since 1754. It so happened that George Lyttleton was elevated to the peerage and he offered William his former seat of Okehampton. (This seat had been one of those purchased by grandfather, Thomas Pitt.) William was elected there on 11th December, together with one at Buckingham, which he gave up once his success at Okehampton was assured.

William's position as Chief Minister in the Commons was precarious, to say the least. It was doubtful that he would be able to get the votes needed at any point in the Commons – he had no absolute Parliamentary majority and Fox would not be supporting him, having fallen out with his friend, Hardwicke. On the plus side, however, there clearly seemed to be support from the Tories and independents. But the most important support he needed was that of the King, which still was not forthcoming.

---

1 Before 1782 the responsibilities of the two British Secretaries of State were divided along geographic lines. The Southern Department, the more senior of the two, was responsible for Southern England, Wales, Ireland, the American Colonies (until 1768) and relations with the Roman Catholic and Muslim states of Europe.

His gout continued to cause problems. He was laid up at Hayes during November 1756 and had not been able to attend the King until 1st December. He was then to succumb once more, with the nation's business being carried out at Hayes from December 1756 through to February 1757. In fact, he did not attend the House from the time of his appointment until the late winter/ early spring of 1757 because of his gout.

This did not mean, however, that government had come to a halt. Visitors to Hayes were numerous, with the route between Westminster and Hayes becoming almost a major highway. Memoranda and despatches went to and fro, as did ministers and officials. Meetings of the Cabinet took place at Hayes, one even on Christmas Day. Ayling describes the whole situation as 'a bedchamber ministry', with William, smothered in flannel, either actually in bed or in his chair, and refers to "the operations room of the war and the nerve centre of the nation"[1].

Matters discussed at Hayes, concentrated on war issues, such as:-

- plans to get troops over to America by April 1757,
- to get the Army and Navy in a position to attack Louisburg, at Cape Breton, no later than June, allowing time for an attack up the St Lawrence in New France.
- to put a Bill through both Houses to create the proposed home militia. (The Bill, once an Act, however, wasn't popular and riots arose up and down the country, many men assuming that they would be sent overseas.)
- to put right a shortfall in available naval ships as well as supporting ships.

Problems with the French were also arising in India. The English East India Company, which looked after much of that country on behalf of Britain, had insufficient troops and ships. Additional ships were despatched, but Pitt was unwilling to do more, the situation in America being more serious. Nonetheless, some good news did come from India, when Robert Clive (later known as Clive of India) recaptured Calcutta and the French fort of Chanderagore, followed by the major victory at Plassy.

Meanwhile, in Europe, the defence of Hanover and Prussia's army came to the fore. The Duke of Cumberland, the Captain General and known as 'Butcher Billy' following the Battle at Culloden in 1745, insisted, before he was due to sail to their aid, that a new ministry had to be formed, excluding Pitt. The King responded to his brother's request and dismissed Pitt on 6th April 1757, along with a number of other ministers.

Further ministers handed in their seals of office and, for the next two months, the country was in the hands of a caretaker administration, lead by Devonshire; this, at a time, when the country was at war. Meetings, exchange of memoranda and of letters – some with instructions to be burnt

1 Ayling p.190.

people jumping sides, rejoining sides were the order of the day until, on 28th June, William kissed hands. Retaining his Secretaryship of the Southern Department – the office for which was in Cleveland Row - and insisting on also being the Leader of the House, an essential position in William's eyes, William Pitt had become Prime Minister (in all but name, the King refusing to recognise him as such).

'Prime Minister' 1757 – 1761

The support that Pitt had from quarters outside the political, no doubt, played some part in this change of fortune. His principal champion, the Common Council of the City, paved the way by awarding him its Freedom. Bath, a model borough and one which could not be bought, was another supporter. William had truly arrived.

Remaining as the Secretary of State, William had no need to stand for re-election to the House. However, he took the opportunity to exchange Okehampton for Bath. He clearly had an affinity with Bath, and the town with him, and it was his friends on Bath Council who offered one of its seats to him. This was to be the last constituency he would represent, to which he was elected on 9th July, bringing the total to six.

The stage was now set for William to serve his country in the way he thought best, with his supporters taking some of the key positions. One lesser post that was granted added a further link with Bromley. Admiral Temple West, Gilbert West's brother, was made a Lord of the Admiralty.

It wasn't long before William faced his first crises on the continent. Frederick of Prussia had been defeated at Kolin in Bohemia; the Duke of Cumberland's Army's was defeated at Hastenbecke and in retreat, while France had over-run Hanover. But worse was to come, with the news that Cumberland had agreed a ceasefire with the French and the neutralisation of the allied army. Pitt's plans to damage the French fleet at Rochefort also came to naught. Matters were little better across the Atlantic,

The news about Rochefort reached William on 6th October while in Hayes. He returned to town but was back in Hayes barely a week later, suffering from gout and feeling a need of country air.

Although being Prime Minister in all but name, William was not provided with a home or office, as could have been expected, at No. 10 Downing Street. (His office, being Secretary of State, was in Cleveland Row.) No. 10 was the home of the First Lord of the Treasury and most Prime Ministers held that position, as they do today. But Pitt was not the First Lord of the Treasury. Hence, he needed to look elsewhere for a home from which he could also do business, and he bought the lease of No.10 St James's Square[1]. Could the idea of living at No. 10 have been part of the attraction?

It was here in St James's Square, and at Hayes, that William often conducted the business of the government. Cabinets meetings were held in St James's Square, as Hester knew only too well – she insisted on being there, to provide William with comfort and support.

Some good came out of the debacle surrounding the performance of Cumberland. Under pressure from William, the King, albeit unwillingly, persuaded Cumberland to resign. The way was open to re-organise the army. Ligonier, descended from a French family, was appointed Commander in Chief; Jeffery Amherst, one-time aide-de-camp to Ligonier, was eventually accepted by the King to be commander of the Louisburg-Quebec operation, with James Wolfe in support, while Brigadier John Forbes, another Ligonier man, was to lead the projected campaign over the forests of the Alleghenies to the Ohio River and Fort Dusquesne.

Other good news, albeit small, was coming through from Europe, with Frederick of Prussia gaining two victories in Saxony and Silesia just before Christmas 1757. Hester, pregnant with her third child, Harriot, born at Hayes and baptised there in 1758, got carried away in a letter to William, ever her effusive self, describing Frederick as 'your King of Prussia'.[2] More good news followed in the new year, with the French removed from Hanover and elsewhere. The French were also defeated in another theatre of the war, in Senegal in West Africa.

With plans in place for Europe, the army, the navy and the Americas and the need to finance the war - and many other areas of government business – William was fully occupied. Although he was briefed on all issues, it seems that his colleagues were inclined to leave everything to William, letting him run the war. Yet frequent cabinet meetings were called, often at inconvenient times.

The eight weeks between 8th June and 25th July 1758 saw major action in New France (Canada), with Brigadier James Wolfe securing a beachhead at Cape Breton and Admiral Sir Edward Bowcawen and Jeffery Amherst taking the fortress at Louisburg.

Bonfires were lit across the country at home in celebration, but this reaction was somewhat premature, as General James Abercromby's forces, on a campaign through the lakelands to the north of the Hudson, were defeated. However. Major-General John Bradstreet managed to reach Lake Ontario

---

1 10 St James's Square was to be the home of two later Prime Ministers, Derby and Gladstone. Today, known as Chatham House, it houses the Royal Institute of International Affairs, from which organisation the Chatham House Rule originates - see Appendix 1.
2 Ayling p.220

and capture French Fronetenac, a small but useful achievement as it had implications for the fate of Fort Dusquesne, on the Allegheny River to the south within the British American colony.

Meanwhile, Brigadier John Forbes, supported mainly by raw American troops, pressed on towards the Ohio, through tough terrain and rough weather, establishing fortified posts every 40 miles or so on other fronts. Suffering from severe gastric problems and a dying man, Forbes reached Fort Du Quesne. The next day, 27th November 1758, the fort was taken, and charred remains were all that were to be found. He renamed the Fort after Pitt, later becoming the site of the city of Pittsburgh[1], left a small garrison and was carried on a litter back to Philadelphia, where he died in March 1759, without knowledge of the acclaim he received from Pitt. Sir Jeffery Amherst[2], following on from success at Louisburg and planning on moving on to Quebec, abandoned that plan until later in the year.

On other fronts, there was another mismanaged attack on the French coast, but the occupation of Goree, now Dakar, in Senegal and the capture of the island of Guadeloupe in the West Indies, were major successes.

These various enterprises lead up to the year of victories – 1759 – although finance remained a problem. Various propositions were made to remedy the latter, taxes on shop licences, sugar, on all dry goods, wines, and hops were among those considered.

The winter of '58/9 saw Pitt again suffering from severe gout, taking to his 'great shoe'. In fact his ailments, whether gout or depression, seemed to be occurring with ever-increasing frequency; but he did not allow them to interfere unduly with the task at hand, dismissing his complaints as something that would blow over.

In addition to his own physical, and mental problems at this time, some members of his family did little to help. His sister, Elizabeth or Betty, who lived for a time in France and who he supported to the tune of £100 a year, was assumed to suffer from the family 'madness' as well as nymphomania. She had been promised a further £100 a year by William, on the presumption that she behaved herself. She failed to do so, and went so far as to release William's letters to her to the press, in the hope that he would be put in a bad light. Not only did she not receive the extra £100 but, in 1761, lost the original £100, when she married, at the age of fifty, a youngish man named John Hannan. William had nothing more to do with her.

His favourite sister, Ann, had not helped matters either when, in 1756, she had taken herself off to France, requiring William to arrange to have her brought

---

1 The founding of Pittsburgh is taken from that day in November 1758, making 27th November 2008 its 250th anniversary, For more information see Appendix 2
2 Another local man, born at Riverhead, near Sevenoaks.

home, due to the war. On her return she went immediately to Pitt's villa at Hayes, according to her nephew Thomas, later 1st Lord Camelford, 'where though her spirits were still weak, she was surprisingly recovered'[1].

But all wasn't settled with Ann. Taking herself off to Bath, intending to stay in William's house in The Circus, she soon heard from Hester that she and William were not happy for her to do so, advising her to take one of those 'commodious lodgings which Bath affords'[2]. This she did, but not for long. She returned to London in 1759, staying at various houses. None of this pleased William and aroused further disagreement between them. For a while she lived near to Horace Walpole but moved to Kensington. Few letters from thereon passed between her and William. By the time Chatham died in 1788, Walpole said that she was already 'in a very wild way'[3]. By 1779 she was under restraint and died two years later in one of Dr Duffell's homes for the 'mentally disturbed'.

Not all was doom and gloom within the family. William remained on good terms with his youngest sister, Mary, probably because she was of a personality less lively than that shared by him, Elizabeth and Ann, and thus much easier to handle. Mary never married.

Despite the disagreements, rows even, William clearly showed a strong sense of family responsibility. From an early age he had acted promptly in support of nephew, Thomas, and had provided an income for at least some of his sisters and provided his sister, Ann, with a home, from time to time. His approach to his siblings and their off-spring was generally a kind and positive one, unlike that of his late father, Robert.

At the same time the Pitt family continued to grow. Having already given birth to John and Harriot, Hester gave birth at Hayes Place to their second son, William on 28th May 1759.

While William was devoted to his children, describing them variously as his 'infantry', 'his little tribe' and the 'dear infants', he could not tolerate their liveliness. He, therefore, made sure that the domestic arrangements at Hayes were such that he and the children could lead separate lives. As Hayes was undergoing major works, it was possible to achieve this. Horace Walpole described the situation well. 'His children he could not bear under the same roof, nor communications from room to room, nor whatever he thought promoted noise. A winding passage between his house and children was built with the same view.[4]'

---

1 Rosebery p.103
2 Ayling p.251
3 ibid
4 Ayling p.249

As mentioned already, the house at Bath was rarely used at this time. And, when he needed to relax, whether for a few days or even just for a few hours, he retired to Hayes Place, spending a great deal of time in the garden.

The house was becoming a fine residence[1] and there he could find peace, not least with his beloved Hester. But Hester did not confine herself to Hayes. She needed to be with him at 10 St James's Square, to provide him with comforts and support. Cabinet meetings were held there, even though it was their home, rather that an the office in Cleveland Row. On one such occasion she wrote that the meetings "which always engrosse my apartments and banish me to other quarters"[2].

Wherever she was, whether at Hayes or with her brothers at Stowe or Wotton, frequent messages were despatched by William via one of his grooms, writing sweet nothings or providing her with the latest news of the war, and pleading with her for details of all that was happening around her. Their need to be in contact with each other was very obvious, and kept his grooms constantly busy.

It was beginning to look as though the small successes achieved abroad so far were to be all that would be gained. Even William was beginning to imply in July 1759 that this was the case, suggesting that a peace might be based on them. And the omens were not good; troops in Germany were retreating; there was a possibility that Spain might side with France; Frederick of Prussia, an ally, had been defeated at Kunersdorf and the French were preparing for invasion of Britain.

In response to these events, Pitt acted. The result was

- Additional regulars corps of six battalions of 10,000 men were agreed.
- 5,000 tons of troop transports were ordered.
- Plans for an anti-invasion force were put forward, to be based on the Isle of Wight.
- Some people were allowed to raise and equip troops of their own, leading to the creation of new regiments. By the end of the year some 18,000 militiamen were under arms.
- Citizens across the country were raising money – subscriptions to pay for bounties.
- The Lord Mayor of London started a fund, to which both Pitt and Ligonier gave £100.
- A grand review was held in Kensington Gardens. It attracted so many people that the parade was held up for an hour and a half.

The successes that were to pour in over the next three to four months began with the defeat on 1st August 1759 of the French at Minden.

1 A description of the house and estate was published in the sale details – see Appendix 3
2 Ibid p.247

Meanwhile, in America, Major-General Wolfe, as he now was, was placed in charge of the military share of the St Lawrence enterprise and Sir Charles Saunders the naval share. 9,000 regulars were to be supplied, supported by six companies of American Rangers, 18,000 seamen, 12,000 of them in the Royal Navy.

By 5th August news came of the capture of Fort Niagara. Further developments included the rebuilding of 'Fort Pittsburgh', the removal of the French from various points around the Ohio river and the destruction of French craft in Lake Champlain. Although it was judged that an assault on Montreal ought to be deferred to the next year, Quebec was taken on 13th September.

This major success at Quebec was achieved by the scaling of the Heights of Abraham. Fearful that the British would knock down the remaining walls of the town from the Heights, the French fought the British on the Plains of Abraham, being defeated in the process. However, Wolfe was shot in the chest during that battle and died just as the battle was won.

Sir Jeffery Amhurst took charge of the British troops and the deferred assault on Montreal took place in 1760, the fall of which lead to French rule, outside of Louisiana and the islands of Saint-Pierre and Michelon, coming to an end.

Other successes in India, although not of such importance as those in Canada, were most welcome.

While this was happening, and before the news of all the victories reached Britain, Pitt was again embroiled in what would seem today to be a matter of irrelevance – the refusal of the King to grant the Garter to Lord Temple. The situation almost reached the stage of Pitt handing in his resignation. Fortunately, the matter was resolved by Temple withdrawing – for a while - with the King 'relenting' a while later.

Back to international affairs, during November 1759, there was much activity between the French and British navies along the French coast, resulting in the rout of the French navy on the 20th off the Bay of Quiberon.

With France conceding that Canada was lost, the Seven Years War was virtually at an end, with Pitt , and Britain, the victor – but only for the moment. The French had made an attempt to recapture Quebec but, after another battle over the Heights of Abraham, were defeated. On 8th September 1760, the French Governor surrendered. But the French continued to protect their land in and around Louisiana.

In October, back at home, William and Hester were worried about their two small daughters, who they had decided should receive the, still, risky inoculation against smallpox. Much to everyone's relief, little Hester and Harriot were soon convalescing.

Back on the continent, matters had still not been settled, particularly in Germany. Disputes arose at home, with some trying to circumvent Pitt. In the midst of this, George II died. With a new King on the throne, George III, things were bound to change, for Pitt as well as others. There was talk of which conquests Britain would yield, in order to achieve peace. The 3rd Earl of Bute, a one-time ally of Pitt, with the Duke of Newcastle in the background, was being named as a possible Prime Minister, with Pitt declaring that he would not serve under him.

As the year of 1761 proceeded, the end of the Pitt administration was in sight. He had suddenly fallen out of favour and many were viewing him as ready for retirement. During February and March, Pitt had succumbed to illness, worse than usual, with dreadful gout in all his limbs, and unable to sleep for many nights. He was able to take part, to some extent, in the frantic efforts to achieve peace but, even in these darkest hours, news came of a further victory in India, at Pondicherry, and in the West Indies, with the taking of Dominica.

The end came over disputes with France over the rich fishing grounds of the St Lawrence Estuary. France and Spain were ready to sign a treaty and Spain even threatened to declare war on Britain. Pitt thought that war with Spain was the obvious move to make, but his colleagues' support would be needed. This did not seem to be forthcoming. At his last Cabinet meeting , on 2nd October, he received the compliments of the President of the Council. Three days later, he resigned.

Out of Office

Offers of alternative appointments, such as the non-resident governorship of Canada, and the Chancellor of the Duchy of Lancaster were made. These were rejected by Pitt. However, he had a suggestion of his own to make.

Pitt's proposition was that something should be awarded to 'those dearest than myself'. Any such mark of approbation to his 'unmeritorious' self would be his "comfort and glory"[1]. The outcome of this was to grant a barony to Hester, named Chatham, and her issue, with an annuity to Pitt of £3,000, to be passed on to Hester upon his death, and upon her death to their son John.

Pitt then put in place plans to give up his house in St James's Square. His carriage horses were put up for sale.

His acceptance of a peerage, though not for him but for his wife, plus a pension earned him a great deal of criticism, encouraged no doubt by the Earl

1 Ibid p.292

of Bute's decision to publish details of both, something never done before, in the Gazette. As Sir Thomas Delaval, MP pointed out at the time, if Pitt had gone to the City, to plead poverty for himself and his family, he would probably have received half a million pounds, rather than the £3,000 pension offered.

Matters reached such a pitch that Pitt felt the need to publish an explanation. This in itself was thought to be a bad state of affairs, for such a man to take such a step. Very soon, the tide turned; the City Council passed a Motion of gratitude by a majority of 109 votes to 15 and the City then invited him to the new Lord Mayor's Banquet, along with the new King and Queen. He was persuaded to accept. Furthermore, Bute, who had no popular support, was set upon in the street by mobs, while Pitt, with Temple, and with a little help from friends, was received well.

Pitt was soon to be seen again in the House of Commons but, in the autumn of 1762, he was confined once more to his bed or 'great' chair at Hayes. He was in a very bad way, due in part, no doubt, to feelings of frustration and irritability; eating and sleeping became a problem; the noise of the children annoyed him; he could not write because of a swollen hand and crutches were necessary to walk about. Without the ministrations of Hester, he would not have coped.

With a proposed treaty in the offing, the details of Britain's gains, proved to be over-whelming:-

- Canada, with Nova Scotia and Cape Breton Island,
- All French and Spanish lands, except for New Orleans, lying east of the Mississippi,
- Grenada, St Vincent and the Grenadines, Tobago, and Dominica in the West Indies;
- The right to trade in Honduras;
- Senegal in West Africa;
- Confirmation of all gains since 1748 in India;
- The recovery of Minorca, and
- The restoration of territories of Hanover, Hesse and Brunswick and the removal of French troops from Prussia.

The King reckoned it to be 'a noble peace'[1].

The terms of the Treaty of Paris needed to be debated in the House and there was concern that trouble could lie ahead. However, Pitt was known to be ill at Hayes, and was unlikely, therefore, to make an appearance. Prior to the debate, Bute, on his way to the Opening of Parliament on 25th November, was again subjected to abuse from hooligans. The King was so fearful he

---

1 Ibid p.306 quoting from Sedgewick; 'Letters from George III to Lord Bute".

suggested that Pitt might have to be brought back into government, in order to stabilise matters – an unlikely event.

The debate on the Treaty turned into a major melodrama, with MPs on 9th December alerted by a commotion at the doors to the Chamber. Horace Walpole provided a most descriptive assessment of what followed.

' *The House was alarmed by a shout without! The doors opened, and at the head of a large acclaiming concourse was seen Mr Pitt, borne in the arms of his servants, who, setting him down within the bar, he crawled by the help of a crutch, and with the assistance of some few friends, to his seat; not without the sneers of some of Fox's part. In truth, there was a mixture of the very solemn and the theatric in this apparition. The moment was so well-timed, the importance of the man and his services, the languor of his emaciated countenance, the study bestowed on his dress, were circumstances that struck solemnity into a patriot mind, and did a little furnish ridicule to the hardened and insensible. He was dressed in black velvet, his legs and thighs wrapped in flannel, his feet covered with buskins of black cloth, and his hands with thick gloves .... having the appearance of a man determined to die in that cause and at that hour.'*[1]

Some procedural matters having been dealt with, William, having asked and been granted permission to remain seated, then addressed the House – for three hours and twenty-five minutes. The speech would have been longer, but for William being in physical distress. After apologising for the length of his speech, he left the Chamber, without waiting for the vote, which went against him – not surprisingly. The speech was not classed as one of his best, but he was the only person to take any trouble to oppose the Treaty. His stance, although not agreed at the time, was recognised in later years to have been right.

Another opportunity to oppose the government, which lead later to a great improvement in William's financial situation, followed not long afterwards with a new tax imposed on cider and perry. Pitt took exception to the tax because it was, in his opinion, an *excise* duty, such duties being anathema to the English. He also berated the fact that, in its collection, the excise men would be allowed legally to enter people's homes.

Sir William Pynsent, a wealthy landowner (worth £40,000) from Burton Pynsent in Somerset – cider country - and MP for Taunton, took exception to both the Treaty and to the tax. With William becoming a champion of the cider industry, and Pynsent angry with Lord North, whose wife was to have been his heir, Pynsent decided to re-write his will, in William's favour.

William did not win the day on the cider tax or the rights of the excise men. However, three years later he managed to restore the right of a private citizen to close his door on the excise man.

1 Walpole's Memoirs of the reign of George III.. Vol. 1 p.176-8

These opposition tactics, and others, brought William into serious conflict with his long-time friend and Hester's brother, George Grenville. Hester, as ever, and despite her close friendship with her sister-in-law, followed in William's wake.

Once again, William was threatening to retire, and 'practise philosophy in his village'. Again, no one believed him. His health began to improve and, with the business of government not going well, there was talk of him returning to government. Even the King acknowledged, while he would not 'put himself into the hands of Mr Pitt'[1], that Pitt was essential to the successful running of the government. Furthermore, he called on Pitt to visit him at Buckingham House. George Grenville, who also had an appointment with the King, was dismayed to realise that his cousin was already with the King, recognising the blue and silver livery of William's servants, as well as William's special chair, constructed to take account of his gout. This meeting between Pitt and the King, however, did not have the expected outcome. George Grenville became Prime Minister.

It was shortly before this that the name of John Wilkes came to public attention in relation to the issue of Parliamentary privilege. Wilkes was eventually expelled from membership of the House of Commons, in January 1764, but not before Pitt had attended the House, again on crutches and wrapped in flannel, to attack Wilkes while, at the same time, berating the removal of Parliamentary privilege. It was after that debate that William 'crawled back' to Hayes, ill, where he was to remain for two to three months.

Back in the House in February 1764, William was very much involved in a Parliamentary debate on general warrants, one such having lead to Wilkes' arrest. This debate, like others on *habeas corpus* and the cider excise, brought out once more Pitt's zeal in defending and protecting the private citizen against the might of the state. Over five days, complete with his crutches and flannel, he was to speak many times, at length and often into the early hours, on the last day speaking shortly before the final 5am division. The vote was lost, by a small margin, but Pitt's various speeches were acclaimed by many.

At home once more in Hayes, William was ill and suffering periods of resentful inactivity. His furniture was seen being removed from his house in Jermyn Street – the town house he used after leaving 10 St James's Square – prompting thoughts that he might be relinquishing politics. Even his allies the Whigs, under the Duke of Newcastle, did not understand what was going on, and news was awaited from Hayes.

But William had other things to attend to, not least his house at Hayes. While he was away from the House for much of 1764/5, work at Hayes had at last been completed. The old house was gone and in its place was a new and

---

1 Ayling p.315

elegant house. The grounds of Hayes Place had also been extended. If he was unable to buy a property he rented it, so that he controlled most of the land surrounding the village. To ensure that his enjoyment of Hayes was not unduly disturbed, the closest section of the route linking Hayes to Beckenham was moved further away (that part of what is now Pickhurst Lane, closest to Hayes village). In addition, he had also acquired the manor of neighbouring Farnborough.

It was in this wonderful setting that son William and his four siblings grew up, with the help of many staff. Holidays were sometimes spent in Brighton, Lyme (Regis) and Weymouth. In letters home to her father, young Hester told him that she, John and Harriot preferred 'the sweet chirping of the nightingales of Hayes' to the concert music in Weymouth. Hester also expressed concern about her father's gout, as well as apologising for not writing in Latin – the children's tutor being of the opinion that she was not ready to do so elegantly enough.

By this time Pitt was already regarded as a national institution and wherever he travelled in his coach-and-six, with the livery in their distinctive blue and silver, sometimes with outriders, and sometimes followed by other coaches for himself and his servants, he would be greeted with deference and ceremony. Even the children, when off on their holidays, would be greeted in similar fashion. It was, consequently, impossible for them not to appreciate and understand the importance of their father.

While William was overseeing the completion of the work to his home at Hayes, Sir William Pynsent died and he inherited the old man's estate. It was an estate worth having. It brought William an income of between £3 - 4,000 a year, as well as property and land. But the inheritance did not come without its problems. Pynsent's son-in-law challenged the will and it was not until 1766 that the House of Lords [the highest court of appeal in the land] confirmed Pitt's ownership. But William had not allowed the dispute to get in the way of taking possession and beginning work.

Before William had a chance to visit his new property in the July, the King had reached such a low ebb in his relations with George Grenville, the current Chief Minister, that he made two invitations to Pitt to form a government. The King asked his uncle, the Duke of Cumberland, to persuade Pitt. Cumberland, first, sent the Earl of Albermarle to find out Pitt's terms. Having received the terms, Cumberland, accompanied by Albemarle and Lord Temple, set off for Hayes to complete the business.

Royal dukes were not in the habit of waiting on Members of Parliament, and certainly not on behalf of the Crown, nor travelling in state, with an escort of Guards. This must have been a wonderful sight for anyone in Hayes to behold. But the visit proved unsuccessful, with Pitt declining to accept office.

The reason for this is not wholly clear but it was said at the time that William would not have been allowed to organise any administration he formed as he would have wished; others put the blame on Temple, William's brother-in-law, not wishing to serve in a subordinate position to him.

Strangely, bearing in mind the tension and many disagreements between the Grenville brothers and William, the brothers, accompanied by Mrs George Grenville, went down to Hayes at the end of May 1765, to take dinner with Pitt and Hester. It must have been a most uncomfortable occasion, at least until William silenced George Grenville's attempt to bring politics into the conversation.

By mid-June, the King not comfortable with his government, was once more asking Cumberland to contact Pitt. Nothing happened but the Duke of Grafton delivered a message to Hayes that the King could not do without Pitt. Pitt replied that he would come to Buckingham House but, due to his gout, would need to be received on the ground floor. The King replied, through Cumberland, that he would receive him *'below stairs'[1].

Much was agreed between the King and Pitt at meetings on 19th and 22nd June. All seemed to be on course for another Pitt administration. However, on 24th June, Temple drove to Hayes with the news that he would not be part of the plans. Consequently, Pitt withdrew. The King was greatly disappointed. Pitt, despite the opportunity that had been presented to him, would seem to have lost his chance to be the titular head of government, ie Prime Minister. A new government was formed, lead by Lord Rockingham.

This latest breakdown on the political front enabled William to visit Burton Pynsent. His first impressions were good, so much so that he anticipated spending much time there. The mansion was large, close to woodland and with views of Sedgemoor (scene of a battle in the British Civil War) and beyond. It seemed to be waiting for Pitt's attention and imagination and he soon set to, to extend it, plus other works. As at Hayes, he decided that he could not have the children's quarters too close to his own. They lived in the main house while he and Hester lived in the new extension.

His plans called for much expenditure. Hester expressed her concerns, but William went ahead, nonetheless. The many works carried out included the sinking of a public byway; park landscaping; road building, and the planting of many trees, including numerous cedars and cypresses. However, Somerset did not have the numbers of trees he needed. Some were sent down from London but a great selection of North American trees were shipped across the Atlantic by the grateful people of Canada.

All-in-all, William took to country life enthusiastically. Apart from designing

---

1 Ibid. p.331.

gardens, at Burton there was a dairy herd to supervise and he enjoyed doing a bit of ploughing. He also added to the farm buildings.

Another addition to the estate was the building of a tall monument, in memory of Sir William Pynsent. Pitt commissioned Launcelot 'Capability' Brown to carry this out, and other works within the park. The monument is known locally as the 'Cider' Monument.

24 The 'Cider' Monument at Burton Pynsent, 2008. It used to be possible to climb to the top for views across the countryside but the staircase had to be sealed to prevent cattle, grazing in the surrounding field, climbing to the top and getting stuck!

Money would be needed for William's planned works at Burton Pynsent. Hester had already expressed disquiet about his profligate use of money – which he did not have – and, between them, they came to the conclusion that Hayes would have to be sold. By November, he had a prospective purchaser for Hayes, Thomas Walpole, cousin of Horace Walpole.

Despite variable health, William was enjoying being the squire of Burton Pynsent, and word got about, even to Thomas Walpole, that politics no longer had any appeal, whereas Somerset had much to offer. But all was to change, following the death of the Duke of Cumberland. William, at the time unaware of this, was on his way to Bath.

William was needed once more in government, in particular to handle the problems created by George Grenville's Stamp Act within the American colonies. The great opposition to the Act and the American decision to boycott British goods caused alarm at home. By early 1766 even the King was persuaded that Pitt's opinion on the American question was vital. Pitt returned to Westminster for the start of the January session. The Stamp Act and the general principle of internal taxation by Britain of the American colonists aroused Pitt's mastery of oratory. The debate lasted between six and seven weeks, with Pitt's powers of persuasion and influence, it was said, almost equalling those of earlier years. Some claimed that he addressed the House as if in charge of the administration.

The Stamp Act was repealed and, on appearing outside the House, Pitt received tremendous cheers from the awaiting crowd, many of whom escorted him home as he was carried in his chair.

Hester, meanwhile, was back in Hayes with the boys, under the impression that they would soon be leaving Hayes for Burton Pynsent. Much as William would have liked to be with them, he could not leave London and the House.

On 18th January 1767, the King asked Rockingham to approach Pitt. Although expressing a willingness to serve, the caveats put forward by William amounted to a decline.

During the winter of 1766/7, William stood out as the leader of those in favour of the Americans. The question arose again in the House about Britain imposing internal taxation on the Americans and Rockingham's government, despite Pitt's strong case against such a measure, passed the Declaratory Act, an American version of the Stamp Act.

The American Congress used this Act as a reason later for taking up arms against Britain. Prior to that event, campaigns were started, based on the theme of 'No taxation without Representation', a phrase first coined in 1750 in Boston by James Mayhew, a clergyman and a strong opponent of the Stamp Act and since used in many similar campaigns around the world.

News of Pitt's support reached America and statues to him appeared in a number of American towns. He was becoming a hero.

Rockingham made a further plea to Pitt to join the government. He replied that he would do so only if the King requested it. William again suggested, in the House, that he would be leaving politics, going to Bath and then on to Burton Pynsent. Indeed, he did leave for Bath, while Hester was back at Hayes, supervising the move to Burton Pynsent. William awaited their arrival at Burton, suffering from a serious cough. This had come about due, he claimed, 'to an incautious use of the waters' at Bath[1].

1 Ibid p.347

Pitt soon realised that he was buried in faraway Somerset and became dependant on letters to him for news of London, pointing out in response that he "wasn't dead", In London, Rockingham's administration was falling apart and on 28th May the King, at the end of his tether, accepted advice to ask the Chancellor of the Exchequer, Northington, to approach Pitt.

Pitt was ready to accept, but he decided that he did not want any post in the House of Commons. The situation in the country, and abroad, needed a strong hand, one that was not diverted by the running of a department. With his health also in mind, a seat in the House of Lords was what he thought appropriate. As any First Minister must have a post of some kind, he would opt for that of Lord Privy Seal. All of this was to be kept between him and his monarch, for the time being.

Pitt, on receiving the summons on 11th July 1766, dashed at a great pace to London, arriving next day at Richmond Lodge to be received by the King. He was given a free hand to form a government.

Prime Minister - Pitt's Second Ministry 1766 - 1768

Part of William's terms for office included an appointment for Lord Temple. This would have been forthcoming but, for the second time, Temple vehemently refused, thus creating further tensions within the family. Hester attempted unsuccessfully to calm the atmosphere.

Having sold Hayes Place, William and the family needed another rural retreat close to London. North End, on Hampstead Heath (also known as Wildwoods and Pitt House) and owned by a friend, Charles Dingley, was made available and a lease was taken up. The house no longer stands but a gateway still exists, known as Pitt's Gateway, and the remaining grounds are called Pitt's Garden. William lived there between May and September in both 1766 and 1767. Although he was only the tenant, Pitt had many changes made to the house.

While at North End, his state of mind was such that all manner of ideas came to him. In fact, he was so over-wrought that he developed phobias about privacy, noise and disturbance. This lead to him asking Dingley in 1767 to extend North End – by another 30 plus bedrooms – and to buy up all the surrounding properties. Dingley did as he was bid, at least buying some of the properties, and, according to Walpole, William even moved into a number of them, as soon as Dingley had bought them.[1] Life inside the house also took a turn for the worse. The children were kept away in Bond Street and William became almost a recluse. He confined himself to a room, sometimes not even allowing Hester to enter, and allowing servants to serve meals only through

---

1 One small house on the road currently called North End, has recently been placed on the market as having been occupied/owned by Pitt.

a hatch. It comes as no surprise, therefore, that there is no record that Pitt undertook any works in the garden of North End[1].

Within a short space of time, Pitt had formed his ministry, taking for himself, as planned, the office of Privy Seal, a very light post but a well-paid one. By the end of July, he had been created Viscount Pitt of Burton Pynsent and Earl of Chatham in the County of Kent'[2].

The news of the peerage only became public knowledge on 28th July, as the various ministers waited to kiss hands on their appointments at Buckingham Palace. It caused great consternation, not least because most were certain that Pitt needed to be at the helm, within the Commons. Giving up his supposed title of the 'Great Commoner' was also considered to be an unwise step. His general reputation for independence and integrity suffered and his popularity in America diminished immediately. Even the City of London was dismayed, cancelling at once its planned celebration of his return to power.

Chatham, as he was now called, wasted no time in getting on with government business. He was certain, despite the Treaty of Paris, that there was a continuing threat from the French. To counter this, he sought a triple alliance with Prussia and Russia, but both Frederick the Great and Catherine the Great were having none of it. There were also further disagreements with Spain and, something that brings to mind the events of 1982, he sent a naval detachment to the Falkland Islands, in response to the Anglo-Spanish dispute over rights.

Trouble soon faced Chatham, with disquiet among the Whig factions outside his administration – something he had aimed to push to one side. Threats of resignations, offers of posts to others, requests for allocations of honours were all to take up his time. His inability to resolve these matters were not helped by a sense of disunity within the actual administration, and this at a time when problems raised their head in India.

The charter of the East India Company was due for renewal. While the Company had done much that was in Britain's interest, often with the support of the British army and navy, its servants had grown rich. Chatham was of the view that the Indian revenues collected by the Company should come to Britain, in return the Company receiving an *ex gratia* payment for the administration of the sub-continent. Speculation in the Company took hold and, in September 1766, Chatham announced a Parliamentary inquiry into the Company's finances. Those who had speculated did their best to frustrate the inquiry. There was an immediate split within the government, as well as general unrest at the superior stance taken by Chatham.

---

1 Possibly the last family to own North End was that of the Flemings, whose son, Ian, was to become the well-known author of the James Bond novels.

2 But for the sudden sale of Hayes Place, his title may well have been Viscount Pitt of Hayes. The reason for choosing the name of Chatham is a mystery.

Problems then arose with the harvest, following a summer of bad weather; corn supplies were held back, the poor were suffering greatly and food riots occurred. An embargo was placed on the export of corn and flour, by Order in Council - during the Parliamentary recess. This aroused further strong criticism of Chatham, from in and out of Parliament. The East India business also raised its head once again, while the news from America was not looking good.

The whole situation was getting out of hand and the government was in disarray. To make matters worse, Chatham was frequently ill and out of London, usually at Bath. The King treated Chatham as his life-line and was not ready to let him go, in a letter encouraging him to look after himself and expressing sympathy for all that he must be suffering in both mind and body, an indication that even the King was aware of the extent of Chatham's deteriorating state of the health.

Barely six months after taking office, Chatham was apparently considering 'abdication'[1] – a strange word to use, being more appropriate in the case of a monarch. He set out from Bath for London in early 1767, but he collapsed at Marlborough and was forced to take rest there in the Castle Inn[2] for the next three weeks. Further pleas for him to return, in order to settle the East India and the Parliamentary inquiry, had no effect – he was too ill. Eventually, he reached his house in Bond Street, but very slowly, travelling only a few miles a day.

During that spring, he saw the King only once and did not attend any cabinet meetings. He then spent the entire summer at North End. Throughout this period, Chatham had had to contend with the activies of the MP, Charles Townshend, by then the Chancellor of the Exchequer and his attempts to take centre-stage. Townshend did have some ability but in the May he introduced a tax that was to lead to the loss of America – the tax on tea; his ability to meddle, however, came to an end shortly afterwards, when he became seriously ill.

Chatham's own health was not improving. His melancholia deepened, as did his physical health. Rumours were flying around that he was mad, linking this with the Pitt history of mental aberrations, plus the fact that Dr Addington, a specialist of sorts in problems of the mind, was attending to him. Hester did everything to protect him, as well as helping him to carry on some business, writing his letters when he was unable even to lift a pen. On one such occasion, the response in her hand was to a further plea from the King, who advised Chatham of the seriousness of the crisis that was evolving. The King even contemplated coming out himself to North End, so serious was the situation.

---

1 Ayling p.365
2 Now part of Marlborough College.

Chatham was too embarrassed to have a visit from the King but agreed to a visit from the Duke of Grafton. Grafton visited on 31st May and again on 4th June. Throughout June, William and Hester did all they could to fend off the King, even rejecting the King's offer of his own physician. William's condition deteriorated dramatically. The children were kept at Bond Street. Talk of extending North End did not go further, but he began buying up neighbouring properties as they impinged on his privacy.

William was in fact reaching the stage of yearning to be back at Hayes, having decided that he did not like North End, and acknowledging that Burton Pynsent was too far away.

Hester began to write frantic letters to Thomas Walpole, begging him to sell the house back to them as the whole situation would destroy the children. Poor old Walpole had only been in occupation for about a year and, he too, loved the house. He was persuaded to let the Chathams have the use of the house, but he refused to sell. But renting was not acceptable; the Chathams had to buy the house. Friends and family were asked to help persuade Walpole to think again and, not wanting, apparently, to be the cause of an irreversible collapse by Chatham, he gave way.

While it was known that Hester had, for some time, attended to matters of business, Chatham granted her power of attorney in August 1767. Chatham had always spent beyond his means and it did not take Hester long to appreciate that funds were needed to buy back Hayes. Arrangements were also put in hand to sell off parts of Burton Pynsent. While this was underway, the King, who was shocked to realise the depths reached by his First Minister, gave his permission for Chatham to leave London for Burton Pynsent. After just a few weeks, the Chathams moved on to Bath. By Christmas they were re-installed in Hayes Place.

The journey from Bath to Hayes had required careful planning by Hester. Further problems were arising in America and Lord Shelburne, Foreign Secretary, needed to consult Pitt immediately. In order to avoid meeting him the journey avoided London, as well as Bromley – taking back routes.

Although settled once more in Hayes, there was no improvement in Chatham; he was even becoming confused. While the King and ministers did their best not to trouble him, they were becoming somewhat impatient; even a meeting of the Privy Council had to be held at Hayes, Chatham's presence as Lord Privy Seal being essential. As 1768 progressed, the Duke of Grafton (First Lord of the Treasury) tried to see Chatham, but was allowed no further into Hayes Place than Hester's wall of defence.

Chatham realised that he needed to resign and wrote to Grafton. He gave reasons of health, as well as the proposed removal of Shelburne and Amherst, the one-time general who had become the non-resident Governor of Virginia.

The health reasons at that time did not seem wholly true. Chatham was already in the process of planning works to Hayes Place and had been seen out riding. Nonetheless, the letter of resignation to the King was sent. He resigned on 14th October 1768. He never returned to power.

The Last Ten Years

Out of office and into the autumn, Chatham's health made a turn for the better. A reconciliation with Hester's two brothers, Lord Temple and George Grenville, was also achieved, leading to Temple making occasional visits to Hayes, on which he found his brother-in-law much improved and with a clear mind.

Chatham was again buying up properties in Hayes, this time being personally involved in the negotiations for an adjacent estate. He was also feeling well enough to follow activities up in London, where the Wilkes case was under consideration once more. By July 1768, William was in town, attending the King's levee, and spending some 20 minutes in a private audience with the King.

At the end of the month, the friendly relations between the Pitts and Grenvilles gained momentum, with William and Hester making a visit to the Temples at Stowe, followed by a short stay at Wotton. Meanwhile, work was in hand at Hayes, forcing the family into temporary exile.

William's cousin, the 2nd Earl of Stanhope, came to the rescue, offering Chevening for the Chatham's use; Chevening was the Stanhope's house near Westerham, now the official country home of the Foreign Secretary. The Chathams stayed there for some months and William had an opportunity to give time and thought to the estate – the Stanhopes were in Geneva. Not being the planting season, he confined his activities to other aspects of gardening, creating what was to become known as 'Lord Chatham's Ride'. Young John Pitt also enjoyed his time at Chevening, quite awestruck, according to Chatham, by the size and content of Stanhope's library. As for daughter Hester, she too stayed at Chevening, which was eventually to become her home following her marriage to Stanhope's son, Lord Mahon.

Meanwhile, the situation in America was deteriorating further, with protests against troops, powers of governors and all manner of things which upset the colonists. Efforts were made at home to try and ameliorate the complaints, with the withdrawal of a number of duties on goods – but the tax on tea remained. The Wilkes' affair raised its head once more, Chatham using the opportunity of the Lords' Address to speak twice. His second attempt was on the need, not for the first time, to protect the freedom of Englishmen. In the process, the Lords' Chamber, was able to appreciate Chatham's superb powers of oratory.

25 Chevening, 1989

In opposition, Chatham, with the Grenvilles and others in his wake, was clearly doing damage to the government. He was once more prominent in the new 'war' between the City and Westminster, so much so that his taking of a peerage was forgiven. On 1st June, a deputation of the Common Council of the City called on him, to express its appreciation of his zeal in protecting their liberties.

In 1769, a summer visit was made to Burton Pynsent, with son John and his tutor, Edward Wilson, and then on to stay with the Grenvilles at Stowe. From Burton, he sent news about the 'superb' *cider* memorial. Back in Hayes, Chatham would go out in the little chaise, with William and James in charge, through the fields and generally inspecting the estate.

The following two years saw Chatham in the Lords on many occasions, up on his feet and giving his best. But, from the spring of 1771 – with one exception in May 1772 – he was absent from Parliament for a second period of three years. His attention now centred on his family and Burton Pynsent,

The summer of 1773 saw Chatham, with John and William, on a visit to Lyme Regis, but he missed *'his sweet love', the 'dear girls' and 'little tar' – son James. His love of his family was great and he went so far as to describe himself as 'an old doting daddy' – 'daddy'[1] not being a word usually associated

---

1 Ayling p.401-2

with that period. Young James did become a 'tar', joining the navy when he was 15 years old, under the command of Samuel Hood, brother of Gilbert West's wife, Molly. James saw service in the West Indies but, sadly, he died of fever aged only nineteen in 1780. The two girls, Harriot and Hester, were also to die young, in their twenties.

Chatham had also made good use of his time with the children to help with their education, including the girls. All were educated at home, with no Eton for the boys. More will be heard about young William later, but with one son intended for the navy, the third and eldest son, John, went into the army. He went in March 1774 as aide-de-camp to General Carleton, the Governor of Canada. Being in Canada at that time, John was present at the start of the American revolution and managed to escape only in early 1776. It was thought advisable from both sides in the conflict that it would be in John's best interest to be sent home.

By now Chatham had sold his house in Bath – to Robert Clive, by now Lord Clive – but still had two expensive country estates to maintain. Money was, as ever, in short supply. As early as 1772, William and Hester were not only contemplating selling Hayes Place, for a second time, but went so far as to approach Thomas Walpole to buy it back. He declined to do so. Admiral Alexander Hood and his wife Molly (sister of Gilbert West) rented the property, although not taking up residence. While in this position, Hood acted as land and selling agent, a sale not materialising due to Chatham's lack of appreciation of land and property values. Various mortgages were taken out, on both Hayes and Burton – plans to sell Burton got no further than selling off a few farms, with Hood providing much of the money. Thomas Coutts, of the bank of that name, took a leading role in most of these transactions, even providing a loan of his own. Coutts had to work closely with Hester through all of this, as she juggled with mortgages and repayments. He was most impressed with her abilities and business acumen, describing her *'the cleverest man of her time'. To add to her problems, Hester was driven to appeal to nephew Tom for funds when son James got into financial difficulties out in Gibraltar. At the time of William's death, £20,000 was still unpaid.

The role that Chatham had played during the Seven Years War in removing the French from Canada, plus dealing with the French threat to the American colonies, could be said to have opened the way to American independence – declared on 4th July 1776 by the American Congress - even to have encouraged the colonists in that way of thinking. However, this had not been his intention. While there had been a truce of sorts within the colony, following the removal of many duties, the hostility to Britain remained – as indicated by the burning of the revenue ship Gaspee in 1772. But the government's retention of the tea-tax, and Lord North's interventions within the tea trade, allowing cheap East India tea into America lead to the people of Boston deciding they had had enough. A tea boycott ensued in 1773 and the

Boston 'Tea Party' – when the tea was thrown into the harbour waters - was their real show of defiance.

North responded quite dramatically, his actions adding fuel to the fire. He closed the port of Boston, compelling the quartering of troops in the town; allowed the transfer of Massachusetts' trials to England, if necessary; and removed the right of election to the upper house of the Massachusetts assembly. Pitt took the view that the government's counter-measures were too severe, and too sudden. But the dye was cast.

With concerns about America and France, the latter not helped by the state of heath of Louis XV in France, Chatham decided it was time to return to Hayes, in readiness for returning to the House of Lords. His return to the House, on 26th May 1774, was delayed for a while due to a recurrence of illness. Ministers, aware of his intentions, had delayed the debate planned on troops in Boston, for nine days, giving him the chance to recover. He came, leaning on his crutch and with 'his legs wrapped in black velvet boots, as in mourning for the King of France'. He spoke, very quietly, and begged the House for understanding and moderation. Chatham then returned to Hayes and to bed. Walpole visited him two days later and wrote a very descriptive view of the patient. Chatham was sitting up 'with a satin eider-down quilt on his feet. He wore a duffil cloak without arms...... On his head he had a night-cap, and over that a hat with a broad brim flapped all round.'[1]

After rushing to the House a month later, in connection with the Quebec Bill, Chatham took advantage of the long Parliamentary recess to learn more about the American situation. One visitor to Hayes was Patience Wright, an American artist in wax, who was allowed a number of sittings for the effigy of Chatham, now in the Museum of Westminster Abbey.[2] In August, and again in December, Benjamin Franklin was invited to help him with his understanding of the American problems. Franklin had, originally, been a proponent of America remaining within the British Empire, but that was no longer the case. On his December visit, he brought with him copies of the First Continental Congress's address to the British people and petition to the King.

The Declaratory Act 1776, asserting the fundamental right of Britain to tax the colonies caused further worries to Chatham. He let it be known that he would be putting a relevant Motion before the House on 20th January. He was accompanied by son, William, and Franklin.

Three meetings were held with Franklin over the following days, including one lasting four hours and on 1st February Chatham put a Bill before the House, spelling out how America should be run. While Franklin was full of admiration for Chatham, the content of the Bill was not as he would have wished. Although the Bill was defeated, it received support from 32 peers.

---

1 The last journals of Horace Walpole Vol. 1 p.370
2 Patience Wright's son-in-law, John Hoppner was the author of the well know portrait of Pitt the Younger.

26 Effigy of the Earl of Chatham by Patience Wright, in Westminster Abbey Museum.

The first shots at Lexington, the start of the American War of Independence, were only two months away.

Chatham then disappeared from the scene, for just over two years, except for an occasional appearance, suffering much more than he had in the past from his physical and mental problems. He had kidney problems, as well as digestive ones, never mind the gout and depression. But, on rare occasions, he was able to take a ride. In late May 1776 he returned to the House, presenting a further Motion, which was defeated. Young William was present and remarked about his father's vigour and eloquence, but admitted that his voice was so low that it was difficult for anyone to hear.

A little later, when out riding, presumably at Hayes, Chatham suffered a seizure and became unconscious. But, by September, he seemed to be recovering and by November he was back in the House. Over the following weeks he delivered four impressive speeches. News that General Burgoyne had surrendered at Saratoga reached Britain on 5th December. Chatham considered this to be a catastrophe and North, the Prime Minister, keen to resign, looked to Chatham to replace him.

The King refused to let North go but many within political circles were also expecting, hoping, that Chatham could save the situation. Everyone was expected to persuade him to think again. One such person, the emissary of the King, was William Eden[1], whose daughter came close to marrying young

1 Later a resident of Eden Farm, Beckenham.

William. Although dismissing their specific pleas, Chatham was actually prepared to come forward, subject of course to his usual insistence on his usual *modus operandi*, guaranteed independence of action.

Chatham promised the Duke of Richmond that he would come to Westminster for a Motion to be heard on 7th April. Accompanied by his three sons and son-in-law Mahon, he struggled on crutches to the House. Chatham spoke, and a response was given. He again rose to speak, with great difficulty; but could not stay on his feet, clutched his chest, swayed and would have fallen to the floor, but for Temple and others coming to his rescue.

Dr Addington, and others, came to his assistance in the Prince's Chamber, then at a house in Downing Street. Two days later he was taken to Hayes. He lingered for some time, repeatedly asking William to read to him from the Iliad. Surrounded by most of his family he died five weeks later, on 11th May 1778.

Afterwards

Not everyone looked favourably on Chatham, either in life or afterwards. However, his death was recognised widely as the passing of a great statesman. There was a great deal of debate in both Houses of Parliament following his death, in respect of his passing, how he should be remembered and the matter of the large debts he left behind.

It was Colonel Isaac Barré[1] who brought the news of Chatham's death to the Commons later on 11th May. He moved a Motion 'That an humble Address be presented to his Majesty, that his Majesty will be graciously pleased to give directions, that the remains of William Pitt, earl of Chatham, be interred at the public expense'. This was carried, unanimously.

This was the first of a number of Motions to be passed over the coming days, one of which was moved by his near neighbour, Thomas Townshend of Frognal, Chislehurst. Eventually, the House of Commons voted unanimously to award him a public funeral (really a state funeral), plus the placing of a monument in Westminster Abbey. His considerable debts, amounting to some £20,000, would be paid by the state, and appropriate provision – an annuity of £4,000 attached to the Earldom - would be made for his family.

It is interesting that some four weeks passed between the death and the burial and it has been claimed in one source that Chatham was buried first at Hayes. But no evidence to this effect has come to light. In fact, Mr Rigby, MP, told the House of Commons on 13th May that 'the body of his lordship had already been brought into the neighbourhood of the Abbey'. Since Chatham

---

1 Barré served under Wolfe in Canada, MP, became part of Pitt's 'camp' 1764 in connection with Stamp Act, previously a Vice-Treasurer of Ireland, resigned with Pitt in 1768, one of Pitt's 'lieutenants'.

was taken to a house in Downing Street on the night of his collapse, it could perhaps be assumed that that may be where his body was taken on its return from Hayes.

There had been a dispute, between the City and Westminster as to the actual place of burial, the family having given no inference that it should be either at Hayes or Burton Pynsent. Westminster won the day, to the City's great disappointment.

Chatham's body laid in state in the black-draped Painted Chamber of Parliament, for the two days of 7th and 8th June. Attended by eight halberdiers and ten torch bearers, his body was taken on 9th June from Westminster Hall to Westminster Abbey, in a procession, starting at 10 o'clock, which included 70 of the poor – one for each year of his life.[1] Barré carried the banner, supported by Lord Rockingham and the Dukes of Northumberland, Richmond and Manchester. The pall bearers were Edmund Burke, Sir George Saville, Thomas Townshend, and John Dunning (later, Lord Ashburton). Although the Court was not officially represented, the Duke of Gloucester attended. His body lies in the North Transept.

That evening, son William returned to Harley Street, where he had been staying with his brother-in-law, Mahon. William, of course had been chief mourner, due to his elder brother's absence. It would appear, however, that Lady Chatham was not present as, on that evening, William wrote to her, giving a description of the sad occasion and advising her that it came to an end at 4 o'clock.

The next morning William joined his mother at Hayes and, shortly afterwards, the family went down to Burton Pynsent. Before leaving, on 10th June, possibly accompanied by William, Lady Chatham seems to have attended a service at Hayes Parish Church, as the Church accounts record her as paying £10.10s for surplice fees.

The fees for the funeral, amounting to £301.10s.1d, were received via warrant from Lord Hertford, Lord Chamberlain, on 8th March 1779.

Hayes Place remained in the ownership of the family for a number of years, but Lady Chatham spent most of her time at Burton Pynsent, returning to Hayes only occasionally.

---

1 Son William wrote to his mother asking her if she wished to nominate any of the 70. She appeared not to do so. (Letter dated 6th June 1788, from Harley Street – Birdwood p.10).

CHAPTER 3

William Pitt the Younger

His Early Life

William Pitt the Younger was born "after a labour rather severe'" on 28th May 1759, according to his father in a letter to his sister, Ann, and went on to say mother and son were "thank God, as well as can be". The birth took place at Hayes Place and, according to Lord Stanhope, in the best bedroom. He was the fourth child and second son born to Pitt the Elder (Lord Chatham) and Lady Hester Pitt, formerly Grenville[1]. The Grenvilles continued to be of importance during the son's life, as they had been in his father's.

Hester's recovery remained a source of concern to her husband, as he explained in a letter to George Grenville, Hester's brother, some four weeks later. Possibly due to this concern, George was asked to be a god-father by

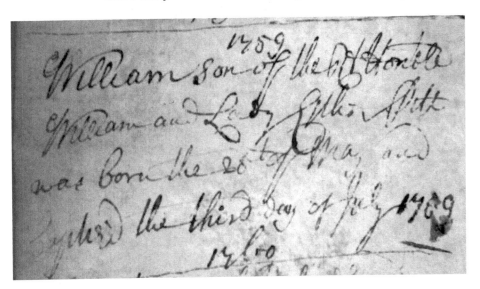

27 Baptism record for Pitt the Younger from the Hayes Parish Registers.

1 It is assumed that the event occurred in the old Hayes Place as the major works that were to see the completion of its replacement took many years to finish.

proxy. William was baptised on 3rd July, at Hayes. The service was undertaken by the Reverend William Farquar, Rector of St Mary the Virgin, the local parish church. Farquar, at Hayes between 1755 and 1774, was not a model priest. He took snuff and neglected to fill in the church registers for much of the time. Far worse, however, was his threatening manner, which extended to brawling in church, striking one of his churchwardens and interfering with the building works of the new rectory (now Hayes Library). The latter event resulted in Farquar being banned from coming within 70 yards of the building until completed. It is assumed that he behaved himself during the baptism[1].

28 St Mary the Virgin. Parish Church of Hayes

It would seem, very early on and for no reason that could have been apparent at the time, that the doting parents assumed great things for this latest addition to the family. He was not only dubbed 'William the Fourth' by his parents but Hester stated in a letter written shortly after his birth "that little William is to become a personage[2]". It may be that brother, John, then about 3 years old, was not showing the characteristics expected by his parents, but William, clearly, was lined up at a very early age to be a possible replica of his father[3].

Much of his childhood was spent at Hayes, a favourite spot of his father's, and at Burton Pynsent, the property bequeathed to his father in Somerset. Time was also spent in the various town houses taken by his father, including, possibly, 10, St James's Square. At Hayes, being within the countryside,

1 Canon Thompson p.64--5
2 At other times William was referred to, among others, as - The Orator; the Philosopher; the Young Senator; Sweet William; Eager Mr William; William the Great. Ayling. P.326
3 Ayling p.248

William was able to pursue horse riding, as well as bird nesting and other rural pursuits. Chatham enjoyed riding with all his sons, although William, not being overly inclined towards outside activities, was less interested. It would probably have been when riding or investigating birds' nests that William became aware of Holwood House, in nearby Keston, which he was to buy not long after becoming Prime Minister.

It was soon noticed that he was a bright child with a great intellect and, from an early age, his father took an active part in his education. This was possible as his father was out of office between 1761 and 1766 and after 1768 and consequently would have had the time to discuss many things with his children. Having a senior and former Prime Minister as one's father was bound to have an impact on a child such as William and important visitors to the various family homes were a common feature of life within this family. As William Hague points out in his biography of young William, "at no other time in British history has the head of one administration acted as the tutor of another"[1].

But William must indeed must have been prodigious. When only three years old, *he was writing to his mother from Hayes, "in his bold, childish hand", apologising not only for his improper behaviour, but that of brother James, and begging her pardon. Clearly, while he could write a good letter, he was also a child who did not always do as others would have wished[2].

William was educated at home, as were his brothers and sisters, as a result of their father's experiences at Eton. Chatham put himself in charge of both the formal and informal side of their education and, following the arrival of a tutor, the Revd Edward Wilson, would assist that admirable person. Wilson was to stay with the family for many years. Subjects covered by Chatham included Latin, Greek, literature, history and speech-making in English. A further element of William's personal education is claimed to include learning to address the House of Commons. There may be doubts as to whether or not Chatham placed William on a horse block to practice his oratory at the time, but there may well be a grain of truth in the story.

There were lighter moments spent with his father, often occurring when his mother was away. Chatham liked to have the children to himself. On one occasion, when writing to Hester about William, who was underweight and of a delicate nature, Chatham said "My account is happy, dearest love. Our sweet little boy passed the night well, and is quite easy this morning, having had, before going to bed, a copious motion. The discreet Pam (Mrs Sparry, the housekeeper) and I agreed to give but four grains of rhubarb this morning .... I have seen the maid who sat up in his room, she says his sleep was perfectly quiet". Some time later, when being charge of both William and James, he wrote to Hester to report "sleep perfectly good last night without the drops, and little James dreamed of no demons, though our *Contes Aribes* [William]

1 Hague P.17
2 Lever p.191

treated horribly of one". This begs the question as to what mischief the three of them, father and sons, had got up to.

The children were with Wilson at Weymouth shortly after Chatham received his earldom. The tutor wrote to Lady Chatham, telling her that William "was not only contented in retaining his father's name, but perfectly happy in it." He went on to say that William had told him "in a very serious conversation, he was very glad he was not the eldest son, but that he could serve his country in the House of Commons like his papa."

William's health during his childhood and youth was often a cause for concern, as was Harriot's. They were both delicate from birth and, as infants, they were looked after by Mrs Sparry[1]. To the children she was known as 'Pam'. As the children came under the supervision of Mr Wilson, he took over the care of their well-being.[2] Fresh air and riding were recommended for William.

The family enjoyed time together, with various ones taking the lead in the entertainment provided. The writing and acting of plays was a particular pastime of them all. On one occasion they performed in a five act tragedy written in blank verse by William, which he called "Laurentius, King of Clarinium".

26th April 1773 saw William arrive at Cambridge University. He was just coming up to the age of 14 – a not unusual occurrence in those days. He was accompanied by his home tutor, Edward Wilson, who was expected to watch over his heath.

But William's health began to fail and faithful 'Pam' was despatched to nurse him. An undated letter from Lady Chatham to William said "I hope Pam will have infused Ideas of buttoning coats, and using particular caution if Cambridge weather resembles ours". In due course, he returned home and Dr Addington looked after him. It was he who put William on the port wine. In the summer of 1774 William was back in Cambridge, fit and well, but unaccompanied by Wilson. His studies were now put in the hands of Revd Dr George Pretyman.

Romance was blossoming about this time between young Hester and her second cousin, Lord Mahon, Lord Stanhope's son. The two families were very close, with Lady Chatham and Lady Stanhope being bosom friends, so a romance between two of their children would have come as no surprise. The young couple married at Hayes on 19th December 1774 and, after the couple spent the night, or more, at Hayes Place, the family retired to Chevening

---

1 Mrs Sparry's role seemed to vary between nurse as well as housekeeper. Another nurse, by the name of Linney, and a Mrs Blackman, possibly a mid-wife, must also have been with the family at some stage, certainly in the mid-1760s. Thomas Cholmondeley, husband of Essex Pitt, wrote to Lady Chatham in 1768 to thank her for recommending them at the birth of his daughter. Lever p. 195.
2 Ibid p.192

Charles Lord Viscount Mahon of [the] Parish of Chevening in the County of Kent Batchelor and the Right Honble Lady Hester Pitt of [this] Parish Spinster were Married in this [Parish] by [Special] Licence at the Earl of Chathams this nineteenth Day of December in the Year One Thousand Seven Hundred and seventy four by me E. Wilson Chaplain to the Earl of Chatham

This Marriage was { Mahon
Solemnized between Us { Hester Pitt

In the { Stanhope Chatham.
Presence of { B.H. Hamilton

29 Marriage entry for Lord Mahon and Hester Pitt from the Hayes Parish Registers, 1774.

30 William Wilberforce aged 29.

for the wedding celebrations.[1] William remained at Pembroke College until 1779, gaining his Bachelor's degree in 1776. There was no need, as was the custom of the time, for him, as the son of a nobleman, to take any actual examinations.

1 The service was conducted by the Pitt children's former tutor Rev. Edward Wilson

Although William, through his various family connections, was familiar with many of the leading families of the day, it was while at Cambridge that he made friendships that were to last throughout his life and which would have influence on his career. One such person was William Wilberforce. Wilberforce, although the same age as William, did not arrive at Cambridge until 1776 after being educated at Hull Grammar School. He was the wealthy son of a banker with an estate in Yorkshire. The behaviour of some of the students seems to have come as a bit of a surprise to Wilberforce, writing that he was faced, on his very first night at the university, by a set of very licentious young men, who drank hard and whose conversation left much to be desired. Whether he included William in this description is not clear.

By the time William had left Cambridge, his father had died and his elder brother, John, had succeeded to the title as the 2nd Earl of Chatham. William, as has already been explained, was much involved in the major and sad event of his father's death. The onus of organising the funeral, and many other matters, fell on to William's shoulders, as brother John wasn't in the country at the time[1]. He spent a great deal of the time in London where he supervised the funeral arrangements, staying with his cousin Lord Mahon in Harley Street. Although obviously very busy, he still found time to write to his mother, every day, keeping her abreast of the arrangements. However, she did not attend the funeral.

William, even though not head of the family, was already showing signs of his sense of responsibility towards his mother, and his brothers and sisters, which was to continue throughout his life. Once the funeral was over, Lady Chatham visited Hayes only occasionally, spending most of her time at Burton Pynsent.

From an early age, it became obvious that politics would play a part in William's life but, even before leaving university, he had decided to go into law, and become a barrister. In a letter to his mother of 10th November 1776, he expressed the wish that she would have no objection to this, letting her know that his father had intimated that he should attend a course of lectures in Civil Law.

Studying for the Bar cost money, a set of rooms being required. On 30th November 1778, while still at Pembroke College, he wrote to his mother that "While I was in town I saw a set that are to be disposed of, and which have no other fault than being too dear and too good. The whole expense of these will be eleven hundred pounds, which sounds to me a frightful sum"[2] Fortunately his uncle, Lord Temple, came to the rescue. He was soon entered at Lincoln's Inn, in a set on the north side of the attic of staircase 4 of Stone Buildings, and,

1 John had received orders to go to Gibraltar during his father's last weeks, and Chatham had persuaded him to report for duty, believing country came first.
2 Lever p.210-11.

in due course, was keeping his terms.[1] He was called to the Bar on 12th June 1780 and he practiced on the Western Circuit.

Having a set of room at Lincoln's Inn was one thing, but the need to be in London also called for a place to live – another expense for Lady Chatham. Over a period of about two years, William's London base was at Nerot's Hotel in King Street.

In the autumn of 1778, William rushed down to Burton Pynsent, to comfort his mother on the death of her brother, Lord Temple on 11th September. Just weeks previously, more sadness had affected the family, this time much closer to home. William's sister, Hester, Lady Mahon, had become ill following the birth of her third child. She did not recover and died on 10th July 1781 at Chevening. Lord Mahon was devastated, but he soon remarried, in 1782, to Louisa, daughter of Henry Grenville, another of Lady Chatham's brothers.

His early Political Life

Although practising as a barrister, William was able to spend much time in the House of Commons, thus keeping abreast of current debates and, no doubt, preparing himself to follow in has father's footsteps. He pursued a number of Parliamentary seats, including Cambridge University and Cheveley[2], the latter being the Cambridgeshire seat of the Duke of Rutland. He was accepted as a candidate for the University seat, but came bottom of the poll. All was not lost as in November, when still only 21, he became the Member of Parliament for Appleby, a seat under the control of Sir James Lowther, a friend of the Duke of Rutland. He walked onto the floor of the House of Commons for the first time on 23rd January 1781 – coincidentally, the same day as his eventual death – and made his maiden speech a month later on 26th February.

Sad news was to reach the family that year, the death from fever of brother James while stationed in the West Indies. He was only nineteen years old. William hurried down to Burton Pynsent to comfort his mother, once more. He also persuaded her to return to Hayes to live, as she would be more accessible from London.

William was described at the time, as being tall, but slight, with the proud, haughty, turned-up Grenville nose. A further description by Edward Gibbon[3] tells us (he was sitting down at the time, eating) he was "a tall, thin, and rather ungainly young man .... There was nothing very prepossessing or very formidable in his exterior, but, the few words he uttered appeared to have made a considerable impression on the company." He was soon to show that he had inherited much from his father, in particular the power of oratory. Both were able to command the attention of everyone in the

---

1 Birdwood p.323.
2 Cheveley, the house, was owned by Lord Granby, later 4th Duke of Rutland.
3 Gibbon was already a famous historian, author of 'The Decline and Fall of the Roman Empire'.

House, although William differed from his father in that his speeches were to show, as Lever put it, 'the brittle brilliance of a well-cut stone'. On the other hand his father's voice 'flowed from him like a mighty current of a torrid stream'. William's voice was soft, but also sonorous. Yet his manner has been described variously as frigid, contemptuous, but dignified and very self-controlled. In fact, he was most unlike any other twenty-one year old.

At the same time, William showed wit and an excellent ability to converse. He had, as a consequence, some good friends. Wilberforce has already been mentioned, but William also had good friends in Lord Mahon (brother-in-law) and Edward Eliot (to become another brother-in-law). Wilberforce went so far as to state that William was "the wittiest man I ever knew, and what was quite peculiar to himself, had at all times his wit under control"[1].

This quartet of young men, along with other young friends, formed or joined an intimate club in Pall Mall, known as 'Goostree's'. William is said to have dined there frequently but this group of friends certainly visited the establishment a great deal, to drink and discuss politics – an enjoyable way to spend an evening which William continued to do for much of his life – and to gamble. William also belonged to Brooke's, another London club.

William's maiden speech was like no other. Most new MPs are nervous of such an occasion and may take weeks, if not months, to gather the courage to speak, and even then the speech is not usually worthy of note. William suffered no such problems. According to Hague[2], William had not intended to speak – the debate was on Edmund Burke's Bill for Economical Reform – so his decision to do so was on the spur of the moment. He also had no notes. Yet, despite this apparent appearance of un-readiness, William spoke confidently, with strong arguments and demolished another Member's case in the process.

The effect of this speech could be said to have been electrifying. Over-night he had become a major player in the Commons. Lord North, the Prime Minister, is reputed to have classed this maiden speech as the best he had ever heard, while another Member commented that Pitt was 'a chip of the old block'. Edmund Burke is said to have responded that 'He is not merely a chip of the old block; he is the old block itself'[3].

William was on his feet again a short while later, this time in connection with the Commission of Accounts. In the debate on the Civil List, he again showed common ground with his father, in that he supported the ordinary man. It was claimed that the Civil List was too high and that it should be reduced, with the money saved going towards the public service. Lord Nugent told the House that the related Bill contained no such proposal, at which point he was 'briskly

1 Lever p. 215
2 P.63.
3 Lever p. 216/5.

swatted [by William] in a manner that became entirely familiar to Members of Parliament over the next twenty-five years'. Horace Walpole referred to the display of paternal oratory, and went on to report that William, answering points that had been made by the Prime Minister, ripped them apart.[1]

Finance was to become an important part of William's expertise, and these two, very early, entries into House debates could be said to indicate what was to come.

More bad news was on its way, but this time news of political importance. On 19th October, Lord Cornwallis had been forced to surrender at Yorktown to General George Washington who, only a few years earlier, had been attached to the British armed forces during the Seven Years War. The Prime Minister was greatly alarmed when the news reached him on 25th November, which gave a clear indication that the American colony had been lost. The way now opened for a major attack on the government and, after the Christmas break, the onslaught continued. William was joined in this by his cousin, Thomas Pitt, with William apparently being treated by other Members almost with veneration – at twenty-two years old! Lord North was unable to withstand the attacks and resigned. George III then appointed Lord Rockingham as Prime Minister, one of the supporters at Chatham's funeral.

The new government was to contain members of both parties; even so, there was to be no appointment for William. It is said that the post of Vice Treasurer of Ireland was offered to him, which, with an income of £5,000 a year, could have seemed a temptation to an impecunious young man. But William was no ordinary young man and, even before North's resignation took place, he had declared in the House 'For myself, I could not expect to form part of a new administration, but were my doing so more within my reach, I feel myself bound to declare that I never would accept a subordinate situation'. The sentiment sounds very familiar.

The first matter brought to the House by the new government was one of Parliamentary Reform. William, an ardent opponent of close boroughs, moved on 7th May that a Select Committee be appointed to assess the state of the representation of the people. The Motion was defeated, but only by 20 votes out of more than 300.

American matters took the lead once more, with the war there dragging on. The government decided to send two representatives to Paris, for talks, which did not prosper. Matters were no better within the government, which called an end to the talks. The country needed a strong leader, which it did not have. A dissolution of Parliament was in the air but was hastened along by the sudden death of Rockingham, the Prime Minister.

---

1 Hague, p. 65

Changes within the new government were soon underway, and Lord Shelburne was made Prime Minister once more. This time the changes would affect William.

Chancellor of the Exchequer 1782-3

William had been a Member of Parliament for just 18 months when, in July 1782, he was offered and accepted the position of Chancellor of the Exchequer. He was 23 years old, and took up residence at 10 Downing Street. He lived there, overall, for 20 years, from 1783-1801 and again from 1804 to 1806.

William described No.10 to his mother as 'the best summer town house as possible'. A short while later, in another letter to her, he wrote that 'he expected to be comfortably settled in the course of this week in a *part* of my vast, awkward house'. The latter comment was made due to repairs being carried out. It was a house that suffered from lots of problems – something that continues to this day - many of them structural, and repairs were frequently being undertaken, some at great cost, so much so that the Morning Herald published frequent complaints.

During that summer, William moved out of Downing Street, for a few months, to make way for the Duke of Portland (PM). It appears that William may have an address in Savile Street (now Savile Row) from where he wrote a number of letters in June and July[1].

The political climate at this time was extremely volatile. Among other things, Britain had lost control of its colonies in America. Within less than a year of William becoming Chancellor, on 24th February 1783, the then first 'prime' minister, Lord Shelburne, had resigned, and the position, officially known as the First Lord of the Treasury, was offered to him. William declined.

A Fox-North coalition government was formed on 2nd April, with the Duke of Portland becoming a figure-head Prime Minister. William remained at the Exchequer. He disapproved of the coalition and declared, as he had in the past that 'I desire to declare that I am unconnected with any party whatever. I shall keep myself reserved, and act with whichever side I think is acting right'.

The following months saw William well-occupied. In May he raised once more the question of Parliamentary Reform, even gaining his cousin's offer to relinquish the family seat at Old Sarum into the hands of Parliament. In June, he introduced a Bill for the reform of abuses in Public Offices. The Bill wasn't successful, but showed the coalition to be very weak.

---

1 Lever p.224.

That same summer of 1783, the Pitt family had, at last, something to celebrate. William's eldest brother, John, 2nd Lord Chatham, became engaged. His prospective bride was Lady Mary Townshend, the daughter of the newly created Lord Sydney, formerly Thomas Townshend MP, who was a pall bear at Chatham's funeral[1]. The couple were married on 10th July and spent their honeymoon at Hayes Place. William called on them, while en route to Stowe, Brighton and Burton Pynsent.

September 1783 saw William set off on his one and only trip to the continent, accompanied by close friends Edward Eliot and William Wilberforce. From Calais they went to Rheims, moving on to Paris where Pitt was a great attraction, both generally and to the French Court. He met a number of interesting people on his visit, some of whom would come to prominence after the French revolution. When in Paris he also became known to Monsieur and Madame Necker, who wished their daughter, Germaine, to marry him; whether they ever offered their daughter's hand is not certain, but there is no doubt that that was their intention. Nothing, of course, came of this and the three friends returned to Britain on 24th October.

Less than a year later, George III, brought down his own government over the India Bill. This Bill had been put forward by Lord North. William had opposed it, in true Pitt fashion, as did others in the Commons. The Opposition lost the vote and Lord Temple, William's uncle, lead the opposition to it in the House of Lords. The Lords rejected the Bill. With the two Houses at variance with each other, North was expected by the King to resign. North thought otherwise. The King would not stand for this and on 18th December North tendered his resignation.

The next day, 19th December 1783, a young MP by the name of Richard Pepper Arden, another friend of William's, stood up in the Commons to move that a new writ be issued for the constituency of Appleby [the seat held by William since 1781] 'in the room of the Rt Honourable William Pitt, who, since his election [to that seat], has accepted the office of First Lord of the Admiralty and Chancellor of the Exchequer'. Never before has the appointment of a Prime Minister been announced in such a manner.

William was 24 years old. He was to be Prime Minister for the next 17 years.

Prime Minister 1783-1801

Politics was very different in those days. As has already been seen during his father's time, with Rotten or Pocket Boroughs, few MPs represented constituencies as are known today and political parties did not really exist. William, although a Tory, was very keen to show his independence, again like

---

1 The Townshends/Sydneys lived at Frognal in Chislehurst, not far from Hayes.

his father, and many of his colleagues across the House were very suspicious of him, and considered him to be 'in the pocket' of the King.

His first administration was also odd in that he was the only member of the Cabinet to sit in the Commons. Furthermore, William did not have a majority in the Commons. A senior secretary at the Treasury, however, with the role that today would be described as a Whip, estimated that William would have a majority at appropriate votes. William, however, faced an uphill task. But the country soon recognised his intellect and ability, and petition after petition was to be sent to the King in support of the actions he had taken on taking control of the government.

Hardly had a day gone by before William was faced with a set-back. Between the sittings of the 22nd and 23rd December, the newly appointed Secretary of State resigned. A resignation so soon after being appointed creates problems in itself at any time, but the situation was made worse in this instance as it was William's cousin, the new Lord Temple, who had resigned. William was disappointed but managed to complete his appointments to the Cabinet.

The Opposition, which endeavoured to treat William as an inexperienced boy, did not wait long to attack him in the Commons. On the day he was re-elected for Appleby, he was defeated five times. In fact, between December and early March 1784, he suffered 16 defeats. But William always bounced back, with the knowledge that the country supported him.

Young as he was, and after only a short time as Prime Minister, William was summoned by the City of London to receive its highest civic honour, of the Freedom of the City. On 25th February the crowds shouted their support as he made his way to the Grocer's Hall but, on the return from the City, accompanied by Chatham (2nd Earl) and Mahon, some of the onlookers turned nasty as Chatham's coach passed by Brooke's Club. It was rumoured at the time that Fox was involved in this attack on Pitt. He pleaded innocence, stating that he was in bed with his mistress at the time.

The Opposition majorities had been reducing until, on 8th March, it stood at only one. William took a chance, a good one as it turned out, and he called a General Election. He had the total support of the King.

The Election was called on 24th March 1784 and Pitt applied once more for the Cambridge University seat. He was fortunate on this occasion and held it with a large majority. He held this seat for the rest of his life. Even better were the results in the Commons. 160 Opposition MPs lost their seats, with Fox hanging on to his Westminster seat by a slim margin. When Parliament returned on 18th May, William had a clear majority in the Commons.

William held an impressive position. The King favoured him, as did the public, and he dominated his colleagues. Lord Macauley, in his biography of Pitt, went so far as to say that William was 'the greatest master of the art of parliamentary government and was destined ere long to show himself greater than Walpole, or Chatham, or Fox, or Canning, or Peel.' Even abroad, his reputation went before him.

Over the years, William had attended various social events and had been accompanied, no doubt by some lady friend or other. Being Prime Minister, however, presented a situation where a hostess was required. William's sister, Lady Harriot, moved into No. 10 Downing Street in 1785 to take on this role initially.

In July of that year Harriot became engaged to William's very close friend, Edward Eliot, the son of Lord Eliot. The marriage, which took place on 21st September, brought about feelings of resentment from Harriot's (and William's) former tutor, Edward Wilson. Wilson, by this time Canon of Windsor, wrote to Hester Chatham, from Windsor Castle dated 7th October, complaining that 'the knot was actually tying without my assistance ..... I could scarcely believe it possible'. Mr Wilson of course had previously conducted the marriage of Harriot's sister, Hester. But, resentful or not, Wilson approved of the match. His letter also said that he considered Edward Eliot to be 'the most promising family man of all Mr Pitt's College acquaintance' and that 'Mr Eliot has everything he could hope for in a Lady'[1].

Within a year, Harriot was dead. The Eliots had gone to Downing Street for Harriot's confinement, much to the disappointment of her mother. (Quite where Lady Chatham would have liked Harriot to be based, Hayes or Burton Pynsent, is not clear.) Mrs Pretyman, the wife of William's former Cambridge tutor, was to attend to Harriot. Everything seemed to go well, with little Harriot being born on Friday the 20th. It was soon clear, however, that all was not well. The medication given to the new mother had no effect and she died five days later.

William, the ever caring son and brother, wrote to his mother each day, faithfully recording his sister's last days. William was overcome by the loss of his beloved sister, although he was able to assure his mother on 26th September that his health had not suffered. She, in her turn, was distraught, often in tears and talking constantly of her daughter. William proposed a visit to Burton to see her but would delay doing so, as he did not like to leave his brother-in-law at such a time.[2] In due course, baby Harriot went to live with her grandmother at Burton Pynsent, which must have helped to bring some light and cheer into Hester's life.

Welcome news was to come from France the day after Harriot's death, with the signing of a Treaty of Commerce with France, later added to by a Convention. William Eden, special envoy to France, was the person to bring

1 Birdwood p.240-1
2 Ibid p.335.

this to fruition. Other matters that aroused great interest and, sometimes, controversy were the trial of Warren Hastings, pro-Consul in India, and the beginnings in 1788 in Parliament of the abolition of slavery.

While the last 8 years up to 1786 had proved to be a most sad time for the family - beginning with the death of Chatham, followed by the deaths of three of their five children - a chance of personal contentment for William was soon to come about. In November 1785 he had bought Holwood House in Keston (spelt Hollwood by William). Holwood had a fine setting, with commanding views to the south to Knockolt Beeches and to Sydenham Hill to the north. It was at Hayes as a child that Pitt developed his love of this part of Kent.

31 Holwood House, Keston. Home of Pitt the Younger.

It is more than likely that he visited the house as a child and he would have got to know the land in between Hayes Place and Keston as he rode about the countryside, Keston being just across Hayes and Keston Commons. In fact, William used to go bird-nesting in the woods at Holwood as a child and he is said to have confided to his friend Lord Bathurst, that he always wanted to call it his own. Plans were soon set in train to extend it but, after a short while, this house was knocked down and another built in its place.[1] Holwood was Pitt's favourite house throughout his first 17 years as Prime Minister, but he sold it in 1802, shortly after he stepped down as Prime Minister, at the end of his first term.

---

1 This house, however, did not survive for long and the house known today as Holwood House was built in 1822 for Lord Stanley.

It was at Holwood that William, apart from extending and rebuilding the house, put into practice his great love of gardening, a passion that he shared with his father. According to Watts, William wrote to his mother from Downing Street on 13th November 1786 that 'tomorrow I hope to get to Hollwood where I am impatient to look at my works. I must carry there, however, only my passion for planting, and leave that of cutting entirely to Repton'[1]. Sir George Rose, another friend, is reported as saying that he had seen William working in his woods and gardens for whole days together, often to the point of fatigue. He also pointed out, such was William's keenness, that the culture of the villa seemed to be the principal occupation of his life.

But the various works undertaken by Pitt at Holwood did not go without complaint, including from Lord Bathurst. These works damaged, in perpetuity, much of the renowned Roman Camp at Holwood, levelling the fortifications. But Pitt 'held in no great respect' the great Roman remains, despite his knowledge and understanding of those times. In fact, Pitt laughed when Bathurst remonstrated with him[2].

Pitt's time at Holwood also saw him acquire land forming part of Keston Common, and other land, in order to protect his privacy. Furthermore, as stage coaches apparently had difficulty in negotiating the slopes on the then new stretch of Westerham Road, Pitt had it diverted, the former route becoming the present drive past the lodge at the crossroads by Keston Church.

Many important people visited Pitt at Holwood, the most famous being William Wilberforce, who made frequent visits to the house. Pitt had a favourite oak tree under which he often sat and he and Wilberforce sat together underneath it on one occasion, and discussed the abolition of slavery. In 1862 Lord Stanhope had a stone seat put there, with the following inscription.

'From Mr Wilberforce's Diary, 1788.
At length, I well remember after a conversation with Mr Pitt in the open air at the root of an old tree at Holwood, just above the steep descent into the vale of Keston, I resolved to give notice on a fit occasion in the House of Commons of my intention to bring forward the abolition of the slave trade'.

The tree no longer exists, but another oak, the third, stands on the same site today with the seat close behind it, at the rear of a public footpath running from Westerham Road to Shire Lane.

Some family honeymooners also stayed at Holwood. William's cousin, Anne Pitt, daughter of Thomas, 1st Lord Camelford, married another of his cousins, William Grenville, 1st Lord Grenville and future Prime Minister in 1791. The

---

1 Humphrey Repton, the famous landscape gardener.
2 It is now known that these fortifications are the remains of an Iron Age fort, dating back at least to a century before the birth of Julius Caesar if not to 200 BC. Philp.

32 The Wilberforce memorial seat, erected by Lord Stanhope in 1862.

33 The Wilberforce Oak, c.1873 on a visit from prominent members of the Anglican Church in Africa, including Bishop Samuel Crowther (c1807-1891) – 4th from the left, a former slave and the first Black Anglican Bishop. By this time it was an important place of pilgrimage.

couple were also invited to stay in Beckenham, at the invitation of William Eden, by now Lord Auckland.

The purchase of Holwood, and other signs of William not looking after his personal affairs, prompted his close friend, Robert Smith (of the Carrington family), to warn him of the ruinous situation he was facing at the hands of his servants – but to no avail. While William paid his servants promptly, this did not prevent them from taking advantage of his laxness in managing his own affairs. Like Father, like son, the scene was set for yet another Pitt to face the debtors. It was because of his financial straits and the inability to afford to maintain Holwood that, following his loss of office in 1801 and to his great sorrow, William was forced to sell it in March 1803[1]. This sale ended all direct links of the Pitts with the area. However, although the house, as he knew it, no longer remains, the seat and a memorial tree remain.

Public Finance, already indicated as a subject in which William had shown to have an increasing understanding soon raised its head under his premiership. The country's finances were in a state of disorder; its credit was low; the national debt had risen. In addition, there was a deficit of £6million and a floating debt of £15million as a result of war, plus the Bank of England was owed money and there were deficiencies in the Civil List. Smuggling also had an impact on the financial situation. William had sought to raise £400k when Chancellor and now, as PM, he set out to raise a further £900k. All manner of items were to be subject to tax but, with the exception of those imposed on female servants and shops, all went through.

Proposals were also brought forward to ensure that the East India Company was better managed; the relevant Bill was passed by both Houses of Parliament, after some stormy objections. The political power, long enjoyed by the Company's directors, was to be passed to a Board of Control.

William was clearly keeping the House of Commons extremely busy, and there was to be no let-up. His next venture was his attempt to improve commercial relations with Ireland, by introducing fair trade, and to tackle Parliamentary Reform. The latter came to nought, which surprised William, and he was no more successful with his Irish proposals. Even with amendments, that scheme fell. This was a great disappointment to William, and a chance to unite Ireland and Britain was lost.

During this period, the Pitt links with Hayes came to an end, in 1789, when John Pitt, 2nd Earl of Chatham put the house on the market[2]. An era had come to an end.

At about the same time, a major catastrophe was about to hit the country.

---

1 His income, as Prime Minister, was around £6,900 between 1784 and 1792 and £10,000 between 1792 and 1801.
2 Sale catalogue details in Appendix 3

George III had suffered various bouts of illness, including what seemed like dementia, since 1765. Although apparently healthy at the start of 1788 – he had even walked one day the 12 miles from Windsor to London – as the months passed, he deteriorated rapidly, so much so that in late '88 and early'89, the question of a Regency came before both Houses of Parliament. Pitt was of the opinion that, if a Regency was required, it should be of a limited kind, with the Queen in charge of the King's care and of his Household. It was expected by some that the Prince of Wales would become Regent, a prospect that had no appeal to Pitt.

William expected the worse as a result of his antipathy to the Regency proposals and began to make arrangements to return to the Bar. News of this travelled fast and soon the City bankers and merchants began work to raise £50,000 for him. So successful were the merchants and bankers that £100,000 was raised. But William refused to accept the money. In the meantime the debates continued. At the same time the King's heath began to improve. By February 1789 it was decided that the King had recovered. The country celebrated and William remained in Office.

Six months later , on 14th July, the fall of the Bastille in Paris launched the start of the French Revolution. The news found support among some in Britain, including William's cousin, the Earl of Stanhope, formerly Lord Mahon. Stanhope, with some 650 supporters, forming the Society for Commemorating the Revolution in Great Britain, sent a message of support to the new National Assembly in France, on the first anniversary of the storming of the Bastille. The President of the Assembly was delighted to receive this message.

Pitt had been facing many problems. Britain had become isolated and various agreements/pacts were being drawn up in Europe. He needed to recover a prominent place for Britain within Europe, as well as restore the country's finances. The Treaty of Commerce, achieved not long previously, would be made null and void by the Revolution. But, by April 1789, he had succeeded in obtaining a triple alliance between Britain, Prussia and Holland. This was considered to be a major achievement for Pitt as it placed Britain, once more, as one of the great powers of Europe.

But William then damaged his reputation by the part he played in the various requests from members of his family for peerages and other like awards. It was not unusual in this period of the country's history for requests to be made for favours and honours by one family member of another. But, having adopted a stance of independence, honesty and integrity over the years, William did himself no favours by putting forward various requests.

Meanwhile, in France, the mob was not satisfied with the changes that had been made within the government. The King had lost control and the mob ruled, for a while. At home, the Whigs welcomed all that was happening in France, while Edmund Burke had forebodings as to what could evolve. Pitt, on the other hand, took a balanced view. Some sense of calm returned to France, under Mirabeau, a man of some ability and eloquence. Mirabeau recognised that, for the Revolution to be successful it was essential to allay any fears of France's neighbours. About that time, Robespierre also came to prominence.

On 18th August 1792, William was appointed Warden of the Cinque Ports and Walmer Castle became his official residence. This was an appointment for life and was given to those who had given distinguished service to the state. Three years later, he was granted the Freedom of Sandwich, another of the Cinque Ports.

34 Walmer Castle and gardens. Official home of Pitt as Lord Warden of the Cinque Ports from 1792.

William, along with the 2nd Lord Granville and Queen Elizabeth the Queen Mother (widow of George VI), was one of three Wardens who had a significant impact on the Castle in that they were largely responsible for the gardens that have served to enhance the natural beauty of its location. Much work had already been carried out prior to 1803 when William's niece, Lady Hester Stanhope, took up residence. Between them they established a landscape, at the core of which was an oval lawn, surrounded by a belt of trees. A walled garden is also thought to have been built in her time. William also made alterations to the Castle and purchased Walmer Lodge for use by his guests.

As Warden, William was also Constable of Dover Castle and Admiral of the Cinque Ports, roles that brought him official duties. He raised a corps of Cinque Ports Volunteers[1] and was colonel of a battalion raised by Trinity House. Bearing in mind the war with the French, such activities were highly relevant and William took to them with some gusto. During the break in his terms of office (between 1801 and 1804), William moved to Walmer Castle on a more permanent basis. No doubt with his military responsibilities in mind, he "peered across the Channel through his telescope, and marched a troop of volunteers up and down on the top of the white cliffs"[2].

The years following the French Revolution brought turmoil across Europe and beyond. On 20th April 1792 France declared war on Austria. Prussia then entered the war, in support of Austria. The French Monarchy, discredited by this time, had to face trial and on 21st January the French King was sent to the guillotine and, not long afterwards, the French Queen followed him.

William addressed the House of Commons on 1st February. He made a strong speech, making it clear that war with the new Republic of France seemed inevitable. Later that same day, France declared war on Britain and Holland. William then set about in bringing together as many European countries together as possible. He was successful, bringing Russia, Prussia, Austria, Spain, Sardinia, Naples, Portugal, Holland, plus some German states, into a grand alliance with Britain against France. This was a major achievement for William, and the country.

The allies did not do particularly well on land at the time[3], although some successes were gained at sea, One of those successes was the taking and occupation of Corsica in 1794, achieved primarily through the determined efforts of a young Norfolk sea captain by the name of Horatio Nelson.

In France, the leaders of the new Republic began to fall apart, with a number of them, including Robespierre, going to the guillotine. Meanwhile, Napoleon had risen rapidly in rank, reaching the position of general by March. In 1796 he assumed command of the French troops in Italy, where he had great success.

Despite the seriousness of events across the Channel, Pitt managed to find the time to form an attachment with one particular lady during the winter of 1796-7. It was even thought that she might have become his wife.

The particular lady was Eleanor Eden, the daughter of Lord Auckland, a government minister. The Aucklands were near neighbours of William, their

---

1 The raising of volunteers was not limited to the coastal towns of Kent. In May 1798 a Bromley Armed Association was formed, in response to a call for volunteers, to supplement the army.
2 Christopher Jones
3 At this time the name of Napoleon Bonaparte first came to general attention, following the British evacuation of Toulon harbour.

home being at Eden Farm[1], Beckenham, a short distance from Holwood. William was a regular visitor to the house. However, the perceived relationship between Pitt and Eleanor reached such a pitch – there was

35 Eden Farm, Beckenham. c.1820.

even a Gilray[2] cartoon about the couple – that her father wrote to Pitt to ask him of his intentions towards his daughter. Pitt replied that there were "un-surmountable obstacles" which stood in the way of a possible marriage. Although never explained, it is thought by some that the state of his finances had much to do with this decision. Eleanor, in 1799, eventually married the widower Lord Hobart. But William was to remain forever a bachelor.

Financial reasons may well have been the soul reason for the breaking up of the relationship with Eleanor Eden. It had been recognised back in 1792 that William was facing further financial difficulties which called for some drastic action. This came in the form of two Powers of Attorney which he granted to Thomas Coutts, to enable the latter to receive his salary as First Lord of the Treasury and Chancellor of the Exchequer. However, his many years as a bachelor could have created within him a sense of unease, even insecurity,

1 The name 'farm' is a bit of a misnomer. The house, according to the drawing reproduced here of about 1820, was a substantial mansion. It was demolished in the late 19th century and the site is now known as Crease Park, on Village Way in Beckenham.
2 Cartoons, many of them very clever, and sometimes malicious, were a prominent feature of publications at the time. Gilray was a particularly successful exponent of this art form.

with the opposite sex, and perhaps he simply panicked at the thought of marriage.

Back on the continent, Napoleon had become the hero of France with his great success in Italy. The Directors of the Revolution had concerns, however, about Napoleon's popularity and wished to keep him out of Paris. But Britain was not doing well, the Duke of York having been driven out of Belgium, some of Britain's allies had made peace with France and the British Channel Fleet mutinied.

Bonaparte, in the meantime, had reached Paris. With the French Directors in support, he left for Egypt, capturing Malta on the way.

Back at home, William brought in a Bill for the better manning of the navy. The proposal was opposed by George Tierney, MP for Southwark. An argument, of sorts, occurred between the two men in the House. On the following day, 26th May 1798, a challenge to a duel was made, which was accepted. Pitt and Tierney met the next day, at 3pm, on Putney Heath. They each fired two shots, whereupon their seconds stepped in and declared that their honour had been satisfied. There were many, including Wilberforce, who were appalled at such an event, which not only involved an incumbant Prime Minister but had happened during a time of war.

Following the many successes of Bonaparte in Egypt and elsewhere in the Middle East, Turkey then declared war on France. However, Napoleon's luck turned and he was forced to retire from Egypt at the behest of a British naval captain, under the command of Sir Sidney Smith, with two ships. Napoleon returned to France, where he planned to become one of the ruling Directors. In fact, a major change in the running of France took place at a charged meeting of the Councils of St Cloud, whereby Napoleon became First Consul of France.

Napoleon then proceeded to seek peace with Britain and Austria. A general peace could have been pursued but nobody saw any advantage in seeking a peace with this dictator of France, as Napoleon was now perceived. The peace offer was rejected by Pitt, with the support of his entire Cabinet as well as that of the King.

The House of Commons was not wholly happy with the situation. Pitt was challenged yet again by George Tierney – but not to a duel this time – who asked him to state, in one sentence, the object of the war. Pitt's response was instant and to the point – "[Mr Tierney] defies me to state in one sentence what is the object of the war. I know not whether I can do it in one sentence, but in one word I can tell him - it is Security! " Pitt continued, including comments such as "This country alone of all the nations of Europe ..." and "We *alone* recognised the necessity of open war ..." .

This stance taken by Pitt will be familiar to those who remember the Second World War, when Britain, under the leadership of Winston Churchill, was left on its own to fight Nazi Germany.

Napoleon soon showed the value he put on his overtures seeking peace, by marching his army across the Alps, seizing Milan and defeating the Austrians at Marengo.

While this was happening, matters were coming to a head in connection with Pitt's plans for Ireland, which would have a fateful outcome for Pitt. In 1795, he had sent a new Lord Lieutenant to Ireland, Lord Fitzwilliam, a known Roman Catholic sympathiser. After various actions on Fitzwilliam's part, he had to be recalled, following complaints. Organised terror then took hold of Ireland and there was rebellion in 1796. To Pitt and others, it seemed that there was one solution to the problem – to unite the English and Irish Parliaments, in much the same as the unification between England and Scotland that had taken place in 1707. Lord Castlereagh, a new Chief Secretary and future Prime Minister, carried out successful negotiations. However, in that process concessions to the Irish Roman Catholics, opening the way to them being able to sit in Parliament, were implied.

Appropriate Bills were passed through both Houses of Parliament, a new Great Seal was prepared, together with a new Royal Standard, ready for the United Kingdom of Great Britain and Ireland. Even the day for announcing the King's new title was arranged, for 1st January 1801.

For no understandable reason, and unwisely, Pitt had at no stage consulted the King. George III did not take kindly to Pitt's actions. And, despite a letter from Pitt to the King presenting his reasons for emancipation and, offering his resignation if necessary, the King would not budge. Pitt responded to this by giving his resignation, once a new government had been formed. Two days later, on 5th February 1801, the King accepted Pitt's resignation.

Between Premierships 1801 - 4

William's resignation came as a shock to many people; after all he had given 17 years of continuous service to the country and there had been no indication that resignation was in his mind. Henry Addington, son of the former Pitt family doctor, became Prime Minister in William's place.

Soon afterwards, William moved out of No 10 Downing Street and retired to Walmer Castle. But this would not be his only residence during the following three years. He remained as an MP and would need a town house. At first he rented an apartment in Park Place off St James's Street, but between 1803 and 1804, he lived at 14 York Place, since demolished.[1] Yet another property

1 The present building on the site has the address of 120 Baker Street. It is also thought that he might have lived at 38 Hill Street, Mayfair, but this has yet to be confirmed. That property is occupied today by the Naval Club.

which he is said to have occupied, and possibly purchased, is that of Lenham Court in Kent[1].

As heard earlier, William's personal finances were usually in a parlous state, and they were no better in 1801 following his resignation. There was much discussion among his friends, including the Bishop of Lincoln (Dr George Pretyman Tomline) and George Rose, as to how his debts could be overcome. The matter of selling Holwood was taken almost as read. £24,000 was hoped to be the selling price, but Sir George Pocock, the new owner, gave only £15,000 for the house and its estate. The complexity of the various debts soon became very clear. But there was some positive news about William's finances - it coming to light that he had given a loan at some time of over £11,000 to his mother. Thought was then given as to how this could be repaid.

William, however, was a very proud man. He refused all offers of assistance, whether from friends, the merchants of the City of London and even from the King. Bankruptcy loomed. Fortunately, a few chosen friends saved the day, by subscribing between them the needed £11,700. At the end of all this, William had £4,000 to his name.

Addington, the new Prime Minister, was fortunate to have a number of major successes come to him in the war with France. A glorious victory was achieved by the navy at the Battle of Copenhagen and the British army removed the French from Egypt.

Many, however, were keen to have a peace, even Bonaparte. A shaky truce was agreed on 1st October 1801, with Britain giving up a great deal. Pitt supported the government, but many others did not; Grenville in particular was quite indignant at a treaty. William, in the House of Commons, endeavoured to explain the benefits of appeasement while, at the same time, recommended that the country re-arm[2]. Napoleon, however, had little truck with the treaty, soon breaking many of the terms.

When not in London, William spent most of his time at Walmer, working on his garden but Christmas 1801 saw him at Cuffnells, the home of George Rose in the New Forest. William then moved on for a short stay with the Prime Minister, who had asked to see him, at White Lodge in Richmond Park. Although William was willing to continue to support the government in its foreign affairs, he had problems with its financial errors. This outcome of his meeting with Addington was described in a letter written by William on 11th January 1802, while staying at Lord Camden's home in Chislehurst.

William's popularity and the respect shown towards him continued unabated. In May 1802, at the time of an Inquiry into Pitt's administration, Lord Belgrave put a Motion, which was carried by a large majority, "That the

1 Symes p.129
2 A possible parallel with the Munich crisis of 1938?

Right Honourable William Pitt has rendered great and important services to his country, and especially deserves the gratitude of this House". This was followed a few days later, on William's 43rd birthday on the 28th May, by a grand dinner in the Merchant Taylors Hall in the City. Tickets for the dinner soon sold out, although William did not attend.

A General Election was called on 29th June. William went to Cambridge, to Pembroke Hall, his old *alma mater*, to consult his constituents. Needless to say, he was returned, unopposed.

Shortly afterwards, William succumbed to illness, much of it affecting his stomach. This was a recurrence of illnesses suffered over the previous few years, although he did his best to make little of it when writing to his mother. During November and December he was in Bath, taking the waters. But he made time to visit his mother at Burton Pynsent for what turned out to be the last time.

Meanwhile, foreign affairs were getting worse by the day. Even Addington was prompted to seek authority from Parliament for an additional 10,000 seamen and the forming of a militia. After a one-sided meeting between the British Ambassador to France and the First Consul, Grenville intimated to William that an offer would be made to him which he could not refuse. The offer was for William and Addington to serve under Chatham, William's elder brother. William would have none of it.

But Addington would not give up. He had a message sent to William, at Walmer. The message, with a view to re-instating Pitt as Prime Minister, invited him to a meeting to discuss this with Addington at Charles Long's home, Bromley Hill[1]. As usual, William put down his own terms. After Addington's discussion with others, the outcome of which did not meet William's wishes, nothing came of the initial offer.

On 3rd April 1803, Hester, Lady Chatham, William's mother, died at Burton Pynsent. She had been a widow for nigh on 25 years and had seen three of her five children die at young ages. For many years, she had had a close companion, a Mrs Stapleton, who gave her a great deal of support. Little is recorded of William's reaction to his mother's death, but he must have felt it keenly. Her funeral took place at Westminster Abbey on 16th April, where she was buried.

A few months later, on 18th May 1803, Britain declared war on France and William made haste to Parliament, after about two years' absence. He made what was described by Lord Malmesbury as one of the greatest speeches of his career, supporting war. After the government won the vote by a huge majority, William returned to Walmer, to 'play' soldiers, as he raised and drilled the Cinque Port Volunteers.

---

1 Now the Bromley Court Hotel.

Napoleon then planned an invasion of Britain, with Kent, of course, in the front line. With assistance from Lord Carrington at Deal, William set about the resistance between Ramsgate and Deal. Often he was seen on horseback, drilling the men, by the end of 1803 he had raised 10,000 Kentish men as volunteers, and brought more than 1,000 into the Army of Reserve. He also gave £1,000 of his own money, which he could ill-afford to do, for expenses.

The late Hester Chatham had had close relationships with a number of her grandchildren, not least Lady Hester Stanhope, daughter of her own daughter, Hester, who had died young. Just prior to her grandmother's death, young Hester wondered, as she was about to leave for the continent in June 1802, whether she would ever see her again; she did not, returning to Britain in the late spring of 1803. Hester had lost not only her grandmother, but a good friend and her home.

Uncle William, however, came to the rescue and offered Hester a home. As he put it "She was his dead sister's child – his favourite sister's child – and she must want for nothing that it was in his power to give"[1]. Hester became his hostess, presiding at his table and looking after his guests. And, while William had a home at Walmer, she became very involved with the garden. Charles and James Stanhope, Hester's brothers, also benefited from William's hospitality. Hester was high-spirited, had wit, charm, and many other attributes. Even William came under her spell and, between Hester, Charles and James, he ceased, for a time at least, to be the austere man and relaxed.

Matters were not improving for Addington and his government and Pitt added to their problems in the House of Commons. Addington, on 23rd April 1804, could take no more and resigned. He advised the King to confer with Pitt. The King summoned Pitt and they had a three hour meeting on 7th May 1804. William Pitt the Younger was Prime Minister once more.

His Second Administration 1804 – 1806

As ever, the task of creating a Cabinet was not easy. Although the King had agreed to Lord Grenville being part of the Cabinet, Grenville refused to join. Furthermore, whether by mistake or not, a letter of Grenville's addressed to William was published in the Press. This caused some embarrassment. William's lot was not a happy one.

Napoleon, yet again, was busy on the continent, boosting once more his ego. On this occasion, on 18th May 1804, Napoleon moved up the ladder from First Consul to Sovereign of the French, under the title of Emperor. One might wonder the reason for the French getting rid of the Bourbon Monarchy in the first place.

---

1 Cleveland 'Life and letters of Hester Stanhope' quoted in Lever p.315.

While the reigning monarchs of Europe were faced with an up-start Emperor, the health of George III deteriorated once more, added to which a vacancy occurred in the Cabinet, which was not easy to fill, caused by an accident to one of the ministers. William decided to approach his old friend, Addington. The pair had an amicable three-hour meeting, at the end of which Addington agreed to join the Cabinet, accept an peerage and become the President of the Privy Council.

1805 also saw William taking an interest of sorts in the Church of England. The Archbishop of Canterbury had just died and a new incumbent was required. At some stage, William put forward to the King the name of his friend, George Pretyman, by then Bishop Tomline of Lincoln and Dean of St Paul's.[1] It is not unusual for a Prime Minister to proffer a name; it is done today, after recommendations are made. But Pretyman had sought the position by making an approach to William. The King refused to accept Pretyman and he and William had a major row over the affair.

With his Cabinet complete once again, William turned his attentions once more to foreign affairs. He no longer wanted Britain to stand alone and achieved a treaty with Russia. The two countries then set out to form a general league of the Great Powers of Europe. They were also intent on creating a force of 500,000 men. Austria and Sweden joined the league and a third coalition against Napoleon was formed.

Pitt might have been busy, but so was Napoleon. Not content with being Emperor of the French, he now created himself as King of Italy. Although gaining some further territories, Napoleon intended still to invade Britain. In a letter he wrote "The English do no know what is coming to them. If we can but be masters of the [Channel] for twelve hours, England will have ceased to be."[2] As is well known Napoleon's army did not step on to English soil, let alone gain 12 hours of occupation.

The British Navy clearly would have a major role to play in the repelling of the French. It was then that Admiral Horatio Nelson was invited to Downing Street for a meeting with the Prime Minister. It was the only time that the two men would ever meet. Nelson was impressed with the treatment he received from the Prime Minister, with Pitt escorting him to his carriage. As the two walked through the house, they passed Arthur Wellesley, just back from India. Wellesley, the future Duke of Wellington, would be heavily involved in the final defeat of Napoleon in 1815 at Waterloo.

Soon afterwards, Napoleon turned away from the Channel and Britain and turned his attention to Austria. After success at Ulm, the Austrian forces were split and surrender. This was bad news indeed.

---

1 If Pretyman had been appointed to the archbishopric, he would have become a resident of Addington, just a short distance from Hayes. The church was shortly to buy Addington House, to be renamed Addington Palace, as a residence for Archbishops of Canterbury.
2 Letter to Dacres dated 4/8/1805, quoted in Lever p.325.

The End

Pitt's last speech and appearance in public was made on 9th November 1805 when he attended the new Lord Mayor's Banquet. Arthur Wellesley, later Duke of Wellington, was also present. The Lord Mayor, in a lengthy speech, proposed Pitt's health as one who "had been the saviour of England and would be the saviour of Europe". Pitt responded, very briefly and softly, that "I return you many thanks for the honour you have done me but Europe is not saved by any single man." He went on, in ringing vibrant tones, much as he used to, "England has saved herself by her own exertions and will, as I trust, save Europe by her example".

Earlier that day, he had written to Nelson, following his tremendous victory at Trafalgar, to advise him that an earldom would be bestowed upon him. [He did not know that Nelson had been killed in the battle.] Pitt then left for Bath to take the waters, but, just into the New Year, he set off to return to Downing Street for the start of the next session of Parliament on 21st January. He was not in a happy frame of mind, having just received the news that Napoleon had defeated the Russians and Austrians at Austerlitz.

But William was taken ill en route for London and stopped at Bowling Green House on Putney Heath, a house he had taken the sub-lease of in 1805. It was 11th January and Hester Stanhope was there to greet him. She was shocked by his appearance and demeanour. Among others who joined the pair were Dr Pretyman Tomline, and Charles and James Stanhope. Although desperately ill, William had short respites and even continued with government business, with some Ministers calling on him. But, as the days went by, his health went downhill.

It was at Bowling Green House, on 23rd January 1806, the 25th anniversary of the day he first entered the Commons, that he died. His last words were "O my country! How I leave my country!"

Following William's death, his brother[1] got into one of the carriages that had been waiting at the house, and took Pitt's keys to No.10. There "he sealed up everything" and locked Pitt's door for the last time.

News of Pitt's death soon reached Parliament and on 27th January Mr Henry Lascelles, a Yorkshire MP, brought forward a Motion for a public funeral "for an excellent statesman" and "an inscription expressive of the public sense of the so great and irreparable loss". As with Chatham, there were some dissenters. Those in favour, however, carried the day by a large majority. When it came to repaying his debts, then House was unanimous in its agreement. £40,000

---

1 It has been said that James, William's brother undertook this task. However, James had died long before. It could have been John, 2nd Lord Chatham or possibly James Stanhope

36 Bowling Green House, Putney. It was here, in 1806, that Pitt died.

was granted towards them – about £2m in today's money. Pensions were granted to Lady Hester Stanhope[1], and also to each of her two sisters.

Pitt's body was brought back to London and lay in state in the Painted Chapel at Westminster over 20th and 21st February. His funeral procession was lead by the High Constable of Westminster, was accompanied, among others, by 47 poor men, one for each year of his life, as happened at his father's funeral. The funeral was held in Westminster Abbey on 22nd February, where he was buried in the vault where lay his father, mother and sister Harriot. The pall bearers at the funeral were the Archbishop of Canterbury and the Dukes of Beaufort, Montrose and Portland.

Hayes Memorial

Over a century after the death of Pitt the Younger, at the instigation of Lady Stanhope, a memorial[2] to father and son was unveiled in the Parish Church of Hayes, St Mary the Virgin, on 30th September 1929. Four Prime Ministers donated money to the appeal.

---

1 Hester left England in 1808, never to return, her travels taking her to many places, including the deserts in the Middle East, where she put her horsemanship to good use, transferring her allegiance to camels.
2 This memorial is one of many physical tributes made to father and son. See list in Appendix 4.

Plate 3 Pitt, father and son in later life

APPENDICES

APPENDIX 1
Chatham House Rule

"When a meeting or part thereof, is held under the Chatham House Rule, participants are free to use the information received, but neither the identity nor the affiliation of the speaker(s), nor that of any other participant, may be revealed."

The purpose of the Rule is to provide anonymity to speakers and to encourage openness and the sharing of information. It is used worldwide as an aid to free discussion, by local government, commercial and research organisations. Meetings do not have to take place at Chatham House, or be organised by Chatham House, to be held under the Rule.

The name of Chatham House and, hence the Rule, is directly linked to William Pitt the Elder, 1st Earl of Chatham, who lived at No 10 St James's Square in Westminster, now called Chatham House.

Chatham House is occupied, probably owned, by the Royal Institution of International Affairs. The Chatham House Rule originated at Chatham House in 1927, and was amended in 1992 and 2002.

37 No. 10 St. James's Square, Westminster

APPENDIX 2
Letter from Major General Forbes to Pitt the Elder, 27th November 1758 – extracts

The taking of Fort Du Quesne and the naming of Pittsburgh[1]

"Pittsbourgh, 27th November 1758

Sir,

I do myself the honour of acquainting you that it has pleased God to crown His Majesty's Arms with Success over all His Enemies upon the Ohio, by my having obliged the Enemy to burn and abandon Fort Du Quesne, which they effectuated on the 25th:, and of which I took possession next day, the Enemy having made their Escape down the River towards the Missippi .... So give me leave to congratulate you upon this great Event, of having expelled the French from this prodigious tract of Country, and of having reconciled the various tribes of Indians inhabiting it to His Majesty's Government.

I have used the freedom of giving your name to Fort Du Quesne, as I hope it was in some measure the being situated by your spirits that now makes us Masters of the place. Nor could I help using the same freedom in the naming of two other Forts that I built (Plans of which I send you) the one Fort Ligonier & the other Bedford. I hope the name Fathers will take them under their Protection, In which case these dreary deserts will soon be the richest and most fertile of any possest by the British in No. America. I have the honour to be with great regard and esteem Sir,

Your most obedt .... & most humble, servt.

Jo. Forbes"

---

1 Various references are made to the renaming of the Fort to 'Fort Pitt', however Forbes' letter makes clear that the name of Pittburgh dates from the actual date the Fort was taken, although spelt 'Pittsbourgh'.

APPENDIX 3
Hayes Place – information taken from the Sale Brochure

Hayes Place was sold by John Pitt, 2nd Earl of Chatham, at auction by Mr Christie on 7th May 1789, at Chatham's home in Pall Mall.

The contents of the house and estate were in 5 parts:-

- An elegant spacious villa, with stabling for 16 horses, standing for 4 carriages, interior and exterior offices, walled garden, pinery, peachery, and about 111 acres of rich pasture land surrounding the house.

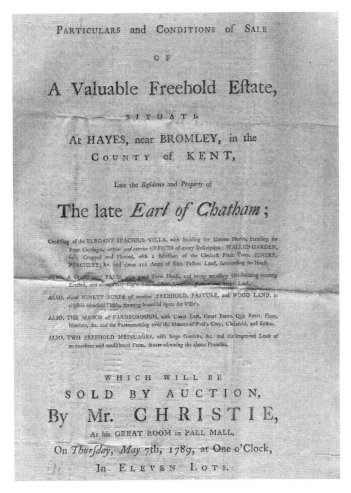

PARTICULARS and CONDITIONS of SALE

OF

A Valuable Freehold Eftate,

SITUATE

At HAYES, near BROMLEY, in the
COUNTY of KENT,

Late the *Refidence* and *Property* of

The late *Earl of Chatham*;

Confifting of the ELEGANT SPACIOUS VILLA, with Stabling for Sixteen Horfes, Standing for Four Carriages, *interior and exterior* OFFICES of every Defcription: WALLED GARDEN, fully Cropped and Planted, with a Selection of the Choiceft Fruit Trees, PINERY, PEACHERY, &c. and about 111 Acres of Rich Pafture Land, furrounding the Houfe.

ALSO, A COMPACT FARM, with good Farm Houfe, and every neceffary Out-building recently Erected, and about Fifty Acres of good Pafture and Arable Land.

ALSO, about NINETY ACRES of excellent FREEHOLD, PASTURE, and WOOD LAND, in eligible detached Fields, forming beautiful figns for Villa's.

ALSO, THE MANOR of FARNBOROUGH, with Court Leet, Court Baron, Quit Rents, Fines, Horriots, &c. and the Paramountfhip over the Manors of Paul's Cray, Chilsfield, and Keffon.

ALSO, TWO FREEHOLD MESSUAGES, with large Gardens, &c. and the improved Leafe of an excellent well conditioned Farm, fituate adjoining the above Premifes,

WHICH WILL BE
SOLD BY AUCTION,
By Mr. CHRISTIE,
At his GREAT ROOM in PALL MALL,
On *Thurfday, May* 7th, 1789, at One o'Clock,
In ELEVEN LOTS.

38 Sales Brochure for Hayes Place 1789.

- A compact farm, with a farmhouse, all necessary outbuildings, and about 48 acres – meadow, pasture and arable. This farm was close to the Red Cow, a pub, which was situated beyond the current Socket Lane. This indicates that the farm is that now known as Hayes Street Farm. The freehold of the Red Cow was also for sale.

- About 90 acres of freehold, pasture and woodland, in various detached fields, forming beautiful spots for villas.
- The manor of Farnborough, with Court Leet, Court Baron, Quit Rents, Fines, Herriots etc and the Paramountship over the Manors of Paul's Cray, Chelsfield and Keston. The manor was indented by George III to Lord Chatham on 21st November 1787 for 31 years at a yearly rent of £1.

- Two freehold messuages with large gardens, and the improved lease of a farm, situated adjoining the Hayes Place.

The house, or villa, which with its gardens etc, extended over 62 acres, all for the personal enjoyment of the family. The house is described as "a square pile of brick building", suggesting that the house with two square, linked buildings sold by the Hambros in the 1930s had been enlarged extensively in the intervening years. At the time of the 1789 sale, the bricks had stone dressing, an alteration introduced by Thomas Walpole in the 1760s, during his brief period of ownership.

The house comprised an entrance hall; eating parlour; drawing room; music room; breakfast parlour; billiard room; ante-room and two dressing rooms. On the first floor there were 14 bedrooms and dressing rooms, each with a desirable convenience and a 'properly placed' water closet. In the attic there were 10 servants' bedrooms and several 'light' closets.

There were many offices, providing the usual facilities such as servants' hall. steward's room, housekeeper's room etc away from the principal apartments. The kitchens, scullery etc. surrounded an adjoining courtyard.

In addition to stabling etc, a coachman's lodging room was provided. All of these were detached and were screened from the house. The current coach house at the junction of Pickhurst Lane and Hayes Street stands on the siite of these buildings and dates from the early nineteenth century.

39 Model of Hayes Place in its final form by Roger Manning, husband of the author.

APPENDIX 4
Statues and other later honours

Statues
Many statues and busts have been made of both Pitts. The two grandest pairs are to be found in Westminster Abbey and the Guildhall. A statue of Pitt the Younger, on horseback, is placed in Hanover Square, while another of him seated, is in the grounds of Pembroke College, Cambridge. There are also busts of Pitt the Younger in the British Embassy in Washington DC and of his father in the City-County building, Pittsburgh.

Hayes Memorial – see p.91

Pitt Banners
The banners, which were sent to Hayes Parish Church after Pitt the Younger's funeral, unfortunately have been lost – possibly having disintegrated. Copies made in the 1920s hang to this day in the Church.

Places
There are many places named after Pitt the Elder, Earl of Chatham, due to his prominent role during the Seven Years War. His actual title came from the town of Chatham, rather than vice versa, but the principal city named after

40 Memorials to the two Pitts at the Guildhall London. The Earl of Chatham, left and Pitt the Younger, right.

him is that of **Pittsburgh** in Pennsylvania. Pittsburgh is on the site of what was previously Fort Du Quesne, a principal fort of the French. After Major General Forbes took the fort, he renamed it 'Pittsbourgh' according to his letter to Pitt of 27th November 1758. (See appendix 2) That date is taken as the founding date of the city - 250 years ago.

Other cities/towns in the USA to have been named after Pitt the Elder include **Pittsfield** in Massachusetts, a settlement dating from 1752. Another town is that of **Pittsfield** in Michigan. Its original name is unclear but at some time in 1828 the residents, being so impressed by the oratory of Pitt and his role as a statesman, agreed to change the name to Pitt Township. Subsequently that name was changed to Pittsfield. **Pittston**, like Pittsburgh also in Pennsylvania, was founded in 1768.

41 One of the banners made in the 1920s to replace the original commemorative ones.

There are, no doubt, other related Pitt place names in the USA. It is interesting to note that the names have been retained, even though the British were rejected following the American War of Independence.

Pitt Island in New Zealand received its name indirectly. In 1791, the ship HMS Chatham, itself named after the Earl of Chatham, reached this island and it was the crew and/or any passengers who remained behind, who named the island Pitt's Island. The 's' was dropped later.

Pitt Island in Canada, part of New Brunswick, also was named after Pitt the Elder.

Streets and Buildings
First and foremost are the roads named after the family in Hayes. **Pittsmead Avenue** and **Chatham Avenue** are the most obvious but there is also a **Stanhope Avenue**. These roads were built in the 1930s, after Hayes Place was sold by the Hambros, the banking family, and the estate developed by Henry Boot.[1]

---

1 For more information about the developers who built the houses of Hayes between the wars see The Hayes Village Association, Golden Jubilee exhibition souvenir guide (1983); in Bromley Local Studies Library.

42 Chatham Avenue, Hayes

43 Pitts Head Mews, Mayfair

Other named roads are to be found in central London, some just off Park Lane. **Pitts Head Mews** is off Park Lane, by the side of the Hilton Hotel. The name of Stanhope abounds across London but **Stanhope Gate** and **Stanhope Row** are close by Pitts Head Mews.

Pubs are favourite buildings to name after famous people, often kings. There is an **Earl of Chatham** in Thomas Street, Woolwich.

44 Earl of Chatham PH, Woolwich

Chatham House, 10 St James's Square, is the one-time home of Pitt the Elder when he was first Prime Minister. It is currently occupied by the Royal Institute of International Affairs. This house has given its name to the **Chatham House Rule**.

School House Names
Stowe, the independent school and former home of Lord Cobham, has a house called Chatham. Much closer to home, Hayes Primary School also has a house similarly named.

Plaques

Four buildings in Greater London are known to have plaques (mainly blue) to mark that one of the Pitts lived there. These are Chatham House, 10 St James's Square; 120 Baker Street (formerly 14 York Place), the Pitt Archway (the only part of North End House, Hampstead left standing) and at 44 Merryhills Drive, N2, by Enfield Chase (which stands on the site of South Lodge). A further plaque was unveiled by the Salisbury Civic Society in 2008 to mark the visits of Pitt the Elder, when a boy, to Mawarden Court.

A plaque to both Pitts is to be installed in Hayes in 2009 by Bromley Council.

45 Plaque at 120 Baker Street, London.

46 Plaque at Mawarden Court.

Other Items

Various items of furniture are to be found at Walmer Castle and the desk used by William Pitt the Younger when Prime Minister is to be found at No. 10 Downing Street.

The City of Pittsburgh adopted the elder Pitt's Coat of Arms[1] for its seal and in the middle of the last century added his motto, "Benigno Numine" which translates as "By the favour of the heavens".

The above references do not attempt to be a complete list of known statues etc. and, no doubt, there are other items that have yet to come to light. The Local Studies Department of the London Borough of Bromley would welcome any information about them. Email: localstudies.library@bromley.gov.uk.

1 Demorest, Rose *'The Point: William Pitt'* in Carnegie Magazne, October 1950.

APPENDIX 5
Some Interesting facts about William Pitt the Younger

- He is one of the youngest MPs to sit in the House of Commons, being just over 21 at the time.

- He became Chancellor of the Exchequer when only 23 years old.

- He is Britain's youngest ever Prime Minister, taking on the great office at the age of 24.

- His time in Office as Prime Minister – 19 years over two terms – is second only to Robert Walpole (21 years between 1721 and 1742).

- He presented at least 22 budgets during his time in Office and cleared the national Debt.

- He introduced income tax as well as paper money.

- He saw through the Union with Ireland.

- He became the Warden of the Cinque Ports.

- Only 7 commoners have ever received a state funeral , two of them being the father and son, Chatham and Pitt the Younger.

SOURCES & BIBLIOGRAPHY

A

Alberts, Robert C
The Shaping of the Point: Pittsburgh's Renaissance Park
University of Pittsburgh Press, 1980

Ayling, Stanley
The Elder Pitt. Collins. London, 1976

D

Demorest, Rose
The Point: William Pitt in Carnegie Magazine, October 1950

Dictionary of National Biography
Various entries

E

English Heritage & Gibbs, Liv
Conservation Area of Walmer - extract from Conservation Statement - [n.d.]

Evans, Eric J
Wm Pitt the Younger (Lancaster pamphlets) Routledge, 1999

F

Ford, David Nash
Royal Berkshire History website. See note on page 11 for full reference.

G

Gerhold, Dorian
Villas and Mansions of Roehampton & Putney Heath
Wandsworth Historical Society, 1997

H

Hague, William
William Pitt the Younger. HarperCollins, 2004

Hamilton-Bradbury, MJ
The History of Wildwoods, Pitt's House in Hampstead.
Camden Local History Society, Camden History review No. 16. 1989

Horsburgh, ELS
Bromley: from earliest times to the present century. Hodder & Stoughton, 1929

Houses of Parliament
Parliamentary History Vol.19 17-19 Geo 3 col. 1224-1255
Debates 1st Series Vol.6 Geo 3 col. 41-73 &128-140

I

Inman, Eric & Tonkin, Nancy · · · Beckenham. 2nd ed. Phillimore, 2002

J

James, Alfred Proctor · · · Decision at the Forks in Drums in the Forest. Historical Society of Western Pennsylvania, 1958

Jones, Christopher · · · No 10 Downing Street: the story of a house. BBC Books, 1985

K

Kadwell, Charles · · · Portfolio of Hayes, various dates (Bromley Archives P/180/28/13)

L

Lever, Tresham · · · The House of Pitt. John Murray, London 1947

Loose, Jacqueline · · · Duels and Duelling: affairs of honour around the Wandsworth area. Wandsworth Council, 1983

Lorant, Stephan · · · Pittsburgh: The story of an Avenue City Derrydale Press, 1989

M

Metaxas, Eric · · · Amazing Grace. Monarch, 2007

Muir, Ian & Manning, Pat · · · The book of Monks Orchard & Eden Park. Halsgrove, 2004

N

National Trust · · · Stowe – Landscape Gardens

Newman, Aubrey · · · The Stanhopes of Chevening. Macmillan, 1969

P

Philp, Brian · · · Caesar's Camp - Holwood Seismograph Services, [n.d.]

R

Roseberry, Lord · · · Chatham, his early life & Connections. A.L. Humphreys, 1910

S

Sedgewick · · · (See p 44)

Seldon, Anthony · · · No 10 Downing Street, The Illustrated History. Harper Collins, 1999.

Sheppard, FHW · · · Survey of London (Vols 31 & 32), Athlone Press, 1963

Stotz, Charles Morse	Outposts of the War for Empire. Historical Society of Western Pennysylvania, University of Pittsburgh Press, 2005
Symes, Michael	Wm Pitt the Elder: The Gran Mago of Landscape Gardening in Garden History, Vol. 24 No. 1 (Summer 1996)

T

Thompson, Canon	A History of Hayes in the county of Kent. Lovat Dickson & Thompson, 1935

U

Ulph, Colin	150 not out, Story of the Paymaster General's Office 1836 – 1986. H.M. Paymasters Office, 1985.

W

Wade, Christopher	Hampstead Past. Historical Publications, 1989.
Warren, Frank	Addington – a history. Phillimore, 1984.
Watts, MC	The Holwood Estate, Keston in Bromley Local History No.1, Local History Society for LB Bromley, 1976
Wells, Hester	John Till of Hayes in Bromley Local History No.3, Local History Society for LB Bromley. 1978

ILLUSTRATIONS & PLATES

All pictures are from the collections of Bromley Libraries unless otherwise stated,

1. Boconnoc House (Fortescue family/Boconnoc Estate)
2. The Down House, Blandford St Mary
3. Robert Pitt (Fortescue family/Boconnoc Estate)
4. Harriet Pitt (nee Villiers) (Fortescue family/Boconnoc Estate)
5. 28 Golden Square
6. Typical House in Golden Square
7. Cutting from the Kadwell Portfolio (Bromley Archives Ref P/180//28/13)
8. Extract from the Baptism registers of St. James's Church, Piccadilly (Westminster City Archives/ St. James's Church, Piccadilly)
9. Mawarden Court, Stratford sub Castle. 2008
10. Old Sarum Castle, 2008.
11. Memorial to the Old Sarum Parliament Tree.
12. Stowe House, main front, 2008.
13. Stowe House Cricket Ground, 2008
14. Stowe House Gardens, 2008
15. Paymaster General's House, 2008
16. South Lodge, Enfield Chase (Enfield Libraries)
17. No.8, The Circus, Bath, 2008
18. Stone House, Mount Ephraim, Tunbridge Wells, 2008
19. Wotton House, Bucks. (Buckinghamshire County Museum)
20. Pitts Marriage Licence (St. James's Church, Piccadilly/Lambeth Palace)
21. Grove House (Ravenswood), West Wickham. (F8/149)
22. Hayes Place. (Bromley Archives Ref P/180//28/13)
23. Elizabeth Montague from the Kadwell Portfolio. (Bromley Archives Ref P/180//28/13)
24. Cider Monument, Burton Pynsent.
25 Chevening (Z/CHE/2) : (Courtesy of Lesley Peters)
26. Effigy of the Earl of Chatham (Dean and Chapter of Westminster)
27. Baptism Entry of Pitt the Younger (Bromley Archives P/180/1/2)
28. St. Mary the Virgin Church, Hayes, 1786, from the Kadwell Portfolio (Bromley Archives Ref P/180//28/13)
29. Marriage entry for Lord Mahon from the Hayes Parish Registers (Bromley Archives P/180/1/2)
30. William Wilberforce (Wilberforce House Museum/Hull City Council)
31. Holwood House, Keston
32. Wilberforce Memorial Seat
33. Wilberforce Oak (K11/30)
34. Walmer Castle and gardens (English Heritage)
35. Eden Farm, Beckenham
36. Bowling Green House, Putney (Lambeth Archives)

Plates (All from the Kadwell Portfolio Bromley Archives Ref P/180/28/13

ACKNOWLEDGEMENTS

I take this opportunity to thank Simon Finch of Bromley Local Studies for his particular help and guidance, and for the assistance given by Christine Reynolds of Westminister Abbey Archives, Alison Kenney of City of Westminster Archives, the archive and library staff of London Boroughs of Camden, Enfield, Lambeth and Wandsworth, Guildhall Library, Houses of Parliament Archives, Lambeth Palace Archives, Mrs Fortescue of Boconnoc, the staff of the Photo Archives of English Heritage, of the Carnegie Library of Pittsburgh and of the Historical Society of Western Pennsylvania/Senator John Heinz Pittsburgh Regional Historical Centre. My final thanks go to my husband, Roger, for his help and support over recent months.

Cllr Mrs Anne Manning
Hayes & Coney Hall Ward
London Borough of Bromley

November 2008

INDEX

References to illustrations are in bold